Hence My Eyes are Turned Toward You

*Confronting Depression with Faith
and The Prayer of Jehoshaphat*

Michael J Eisenbath

authorHOUSE®

AuthorHouse™
1663 Liberty Drive, Suite 200
Bloomington, IN 47403
www.authorhouse.com
Phone: 1-800-839-8640

First published by AuthorHouse 3/6/2009

ISBN: 978-1-4389-1298-1 (sc)

Printed in the United States of America
Bloomington, Indiana

This book is printed on acid-free paper.

CONTENTS

ACKNOWLEDGEMENTS

The list of people who helped me create this work involves more than those who provided advice about the literary aspects of the effort.

That said, I can't adequately express my gratitude to Mike Smith, one of my former bosses at the St. Louis Post-Dispatch, and Dianna Graveman, an excellent editor and writer in her own right. They read the manuscript, then provided much-needed encouragement and much-appreciated counsel. In addition to Mr. Smith, many anonymous Post-Dispatch copy-editors helped hone my raw writing skills into something that actually can produce a readable prose. To them, I do owe apologies for occasionally acting like they were killing one of my children rather than making my stories palatable.

More than words, this book is a series of snapshots of a life and peeks into a mind and a soul, which truly broadens the spectrum of folks I need to thank.

This journey through depression has given me greater-than-ever appreciation for medical professionals. I'm thankful for Dr. James Jones, who first diagnosed my depression and is one of the most likable and caring men I ever have met. I'm still a tad miffed at him for retiring! But God took good care of me by pointing me toward Dr. John Canale, my psychiatrist, and Jan Chartrand, my therapist. I can tell they truly care about me and my family, and they understand the importance of my faith.

Edward D. Jones Investments, my employer now, has been wonderful throughout this time. In particular during my five-plus years as an investment advisor, I had terrific support and encouragement from friends and advisors Scott Wilson, Dave Grone, Dave Kaplan and Don Kohlman as well as from regional leader and friend Janssen Longenecker. And I can't say enough about the special blessing of working every day with Melanie Relling, who became a trusted friend as well as branch office partner.

Though I left the Post-Dispatch not long after I was diagnosed with depression, several people important in my 18 years there provided care and support frequently in my post-Post years: Mike Smith, Curtis Peck, Dave Luecking and Rick Hummel. The friendship with Holly and Jerry Naunheim provided great moral support.

I have been blessed also to have continuing close relationships with several friends that date back 30-plus years, to time at Duchesne High. I always knew there were prayers for Donna and me coming from Kathy and Mike Huebner, Don and Dianna Graveman, Henry and Margaret Loeffler, Julie and Dan Dozier, Mary and Rick Leach, Laurie and Jeff Strickland, and Lisa Vogt. Old high school classmate Rick Hercules and I took turns leaning on each other during the last few years.

Our extended families have fretted, prayed, listened, supported and wanted to do so much more than they realistically could do. To Donna's siblings Dody, Alana and Shawn; my brothers-in-law Mike and Tom; my sisters Marcia and Patti; their respective spouses Frank and Brian; and most especially Shirley and Pete Petrosky, Donna's parents, and Madge and Jim Eisenbath, my parents – we love you more than mere words can convey.

Donna and I have learned time and time again how much God loves us the last half-dozen years. One of the most tangible ways was the somewhat accidental way we landed at St. Cletus Catholic Church in 2003. We know now, in hindsight, that our move into the loving embrace of that parish was no accident. Father Jeff Vomund, who often has provided me with spiritual direction, and Father Jim Benz, an extremely pastoral shepherd and my frequent confessor, saved us from turning our pain into bitterness.

So many members of St. Cletus have helped these last few years – sometimes with meals (during my time undergoing electro-convulsive therapy), sometimes sharing tears or laughter, sometimes praying. I will neglect too many people if I try to list everyone. But several of the men I have met through the Christ Renews His Parish retreats have become the brothers I never had, truly God-fearing role models of manhood: Larry Boldt, Brian Andrzejewski, Larry Schneider, Jim LaVictoire, Mike Boschert, Mike Sepe, Ed Andrzejewski, Milio Balossi and Tom Moorkamp.

I am humbly privileged to have two best friends. I can't imagine a life without Jean Painter, who listens, prays, chastises, teaches, encourages and who for 25-plus years has done all the things a best friend can do to make life a lot more livable. Thank you, Jean, for your honesty, hope and love.

To Kara, Erin, Josh and Jessica: I won the lottery four times, on the days each of you was born. You are more than my children. I have so much admiration and respect and love for you (along with grandson Colin and son-in-law Donny). My relationships with you are among the great highlights of my life.

Speaking of which …

Donna, you are my best friend and give me reason to live every day. I would have disappeared long ago if not for your strength and persistent help. The day will come when we renew our vows on our 50th anniversary of true happiness together. I truly love you.

Looking back at all of these names, how could I reach any conclusion other than this: My God really loves me. Father, all thanks and glory belong to you.

INTRODUCTION

Until a few years ago, hearing the name "Jehoshaphat" probably would have made me smile and snicker as it conjured a memory of an old cartoon from my childhood. I would have envisioned some crazy cowboy flummoxed once more by that rascally rabbit and exclaiming "Jumpin' JEE-hoshaphat!"

They were comical yet meaningless words, really. The name certainly wasn't anything special to me. His story barely registered.

Sure, I had read about Jehoshaphat in the Bible. I confess, though, that for most of my life I couldn't have told you exactly which book of the Bible contained his story nor have shared any of the details that made him extraordinary. I definitely couldn't have explained the significance of, much less recited, the Prayer of Jehoshaphat.

Now, Jehoshaphat's story is as much a part of my life as eating dinner, showering, taking my medication and calling one of my best friends on the phone.

The Prayer of Jehoshaphat is as much a part of my daily existence as the "roaring lion." That's what I've come to call my depression, the illness that has affected my life as well as that of my family and friends in acute and almost overpowering ways for more than six years.

In his first letter of the New Testament, the apostle Peter wrote: "Be sober and vigilant. Your opponent the devil is prowling around like a roaring lion looking for someone to devour." (1 Peter 5:8)

Looking at my life several years ago, I couldn't have seen anything that would depress me, much less plunge me into the intense hollow of disease. I certainly didn't expect anything at a level that could have turned my family's happy life upside-down and inside-out. But that's what a roaring lion can do.

And that's what severe, chronic depression has been for me: A prowling, roaring lion.

The lion is a regal, fearsome, respected animal mentioned in more than 100 verses of the Bible. David gave the animal particular attention in the Psalms, where the lion represented perhaps the most dangerous living form of earthly evil that could attack a person. The king of the jungle struck a nasty level of terror at the worst and a vigilant respect at the least equal to a blazing fire. Writers in the Old Testament used the beast as a threat beyond anything else the rulers of ancient times could imagine.

"He lies like a crouching lion, or like a lioness; who shall arouse him?" (Numbers 24:9)

Reflecting, I realize that depression had been lurking in the shadows of my life for many years – maybe my entire adult life – and would occasionally growl in low tones, though at an intensity moderate enough that it usually went undetected.

I long have had a passing knowledge and awareness of depression. My mom suffered from a serious case in the mid-1970s, when people still whispered about it as a "nervous breakdown," back when they called electro-convulsive therapy (ECT) "shock treatments" and the world of a mental illness patient could look at lot like what you saw in the movie "One Flew Over The Cuckoo's Nest." I went on depression-alert again almost 20 years later when a doctor diagnosed Donna, my wife, with a stress-related case.

About the time I turned 40, something provoked the lion in me. I probably never will know what created the stir or why it happened.

What I do know is that depression is a real disease, no matter what some might say. American Medical Association policy calls it a "significant illness" and encourages all medical schools and physicians to discern how to recognize, diagnose and treat the disease. It can be scary, life-threatening, relentless. It can come with a pervasive attitude of helplessness, confusion, sorrow.

And yet …

Everyone, including those who have to experience the roaring lion's presence inside themselves every day, should cultivate an understanding that in that shadow, in that darkness, in the jungle where the lion lives, they can meet God in a newer, deeper, more fulfilling way.

By the grace of God, I learned that – and in part I learned that through the tale of Jehoshaphat, who has become a friend, a role model of sorts, a prayer partner. He is a confidant with whom I can chat honestly in my most frightening times because I know he understands the utterly vulnerable panic that I feel. And I pray his prayer. I say it with him, I think, in a personal and cooperative way.

Maybe you suffer from depression or love someone who does. Or perhaps you have gone through something else similarly arduous and stressful, even jeopardizing your very life itself.

Whatever the case, the Prayer of Jehoshaphat can help carry you to a better place.

My hope is that in the following pages, you will find some direction and tangible assistance that you can assume in dealing with the real-life, everyday company of depression. I also hope you will find a way to grow deeper in love with God through the suffering rather than turning away from Him. Sprinkled in between each Jehoshaphat-inspired chapter is an essay that might provide some insight toward understanding and seeking that love. And at the end, there are some suggested actions – simple and uncomplicated – that could help after reading each chapter.

There might not be a medical cure able to completely wipe away major or chronic depression, but there can be a softening and even elimination of the symptoms of anyone's depression over time. The ailment might never disappear, but you can discover ways to manage life with it as a constant, unwelcome though somehow tolerable companion.

There indeed can be a life with depression while you wait for it to fade away. It doesn't have to be – and should not be – a life lived out of sight and out of mind.

Depression is common and needs to be discussed in the open, not whispered or avoided. In America, where any sign of weakness is treated with disdain and where depression definitely is considered a sign of weakness, we need to come to grips with it. We need to learn how to respond to it, treat it, live with it, respect it, support those who suffer with it and those who care for its victims.

Perhaps among the most sensitive things I have discovered during my experience with depression is that it's not exactly easy fodder for chit-chat at the company Christmas party or among friends at a summer barbeque. The disease, at least today, comes attached with a stigma, a sense of disgrace and mistrust, a stain on a man or woman's reputation that can turn an excruciating life into an impossible one. It's for that reason that I initially hesitated when I felt God urging me to tell this story. Revealing to people that you have depression is daunting. Life already is thorny. Worrying how others will respond to you once they hear you have a mental illness can add stress to an already over-stressed reality that by its very nature doesn't deal well with stress.

But the urging of the Almighty God, when He does it tenderly yet so tirelessly, is almost impossible to resist. So whether you are a sufferer of the disease directly, with a form mild or severe, or you are someone touched by depression because someone you love is afflicted, I sincerely hope you will understand that depression is no reason to be ashamed.

I have learned that, thanks in part to my friend Jehoshaphat.

I pray you can learn that as well.

CHAPTER ONE:

MEET A GUY NAMED JEHOSHAPHAT

Years ago, when everyone in grade school was daydreaming about "what I want to be when I grow up," my classroom was filled with lots of future doctors and nurses. Why? Because they help people, of course. It didn't hurt that the doctors lived in the biggest houses in town.

That sounded like a good idea to everyone except me. No one could fool me.

If you are a doctor, you have to be around sick people. Sick people tend to hang around hospitals. My logical mind knew, then, that a doctor has to spend a great amount of time at hospitals and clinics.

Ah, the deal-breaker.

I've always had this problem with needles and IVs, the sanitized smells and beep-beep-beeping machines, operating rooms and blood

– especially my own blood. I fainted receiving a measles inoculation in the seventh grade. Every year through high school graduation, they would give me a note for my mom: "Mike needs his Rubella vaccination." My mom never got a chance to see those notes.

After my first few days of life, I didn't sleep overnight in a hospital until I was 11. I actually passed out when the doctor told me I needed surgery on my nose that year. My nose required another operation six years later. Enough was enough. I returned to hospitals for the births of my four children, to see sick family and friends, to take my kids for an occasional emergency, for a personal test or two – the fact was clear that hospitals were tolerable places to visit but never, ever to spend the night.

So, in July 2005, all I could wonder was what in heaven's name had gone so dreadfully wrong. I sat up in a bed on the sixth floor of the local hospital. I could hear screaming down the hall. People shuffled back and forth outside my door, some of them quivering uncontrollably, some muttering unintelligibly. A man sat at the end of the hallway with a vacant expression. My roommate was OK – as long as his medication was adjusted properly and he didn't skip taking it, he said. Otherwise, the anxiety drove him to consider terrible things.

I knew about terrible things.

This part of the hospital never showed up on "ER," definitely not in all the colorful grandeur I was witnessing firsthand. There was a hint of urine in the air. A shriek from the next room awoke me in the middle of the night. One woman's eyes were bright red around the edges, surely from crying without pause for far too long. A lot of crying happened on the sixth floor. For many, there were tears of unspeakable misery. For others, tears of wicked loneliness – an emptiness that ravaged the inside and an absence of loving human contact that persisted on the outside. Not everyone on the sixth floor had visitors beyond the doctors and tremendously kind people who worked there.

Was this really any place for a happily married man of 20 years, with four wonderful, healthy children; a two-story house on a quiet, middle-class street in the suburbs; a man with plenty of friends, a fine job, respect and admiration? Was this any place for a man with strong Christian beliefs, a deep and rich prayer life, more than two decades of consciously trying to walk with Jesus?

Both of the priests from my church visited me. They knew I needed the comfort and support since Donna, my wife, was out of town – out of the country, actually, running a mission trip in Tijuana.

My dad came, too. Not my mom. But I understood. Thirty years earlier, my mom had lived on the sixth floor for three months. If you've spent one night as a patient in the psychiatric ward of a hospital, the harsh memory will make it difficult to go back.

I actually had checked myself in that night in July. "So, what do you think?" my doctor asked as we sat down together the next morning.

"This is kind of a scary place," I replied.

"Yeah," he said, "I'm sure you're wondering why you're here. You did the right thing, but this really isn't a place for you. It isn't a place anyone wants to be, certainly not someone like you."

Someone like me. That's right. That's what I kept thinking: A man with a life that should have been a source of great pride, a man with a strong faith, in a psych ward.

Isn't that an oxymoron -- depressed Christian?

The doc's words stuck in my mind long after he left: You're wondering why you're here. In a place God seemed not to notice, surrounded by fellow patients God seemed to have forgotten, feeling all too curiously that God had abandoned me both inside and out.

I had to wonder about someone like me, a man who trusted a faith that was supposed to create joy and peace. How did that man suffer from a depression so deep and desperate?

Beginning shortly before that July 2005 hospital stay, in a span of less than a year I once almost downed an entire bottle of anti-depressants and sleeping pills, twice checked myself into the psychiatric floor of the hospital to make sure I didn't kill myself and underwent electro-convulsive therapy treatments that cost me a good chunk of memory and two months of work. And when my life seemed to have turned back onto a more promising path, when the outward concerns had receded to less-imposing status, I groggily returned to that psych floor after an obviously unsuccessful yet clearly purposeful endeavor to end my life and the agony inside.

How did someone like me *still* find myself suffering from major depression more than six years after the initial diagnosis?

Better yet, the questions probably should have been: How did I get through all of that without losing my wife, alienating my children, turning aside my friends, moving into unemployment? How did I not yield entirely to the roaring lion of depression and passively consent as it devoured me? What kept me alive when, honestly, for months all I wanted to do was die?

Please, let me tell you a story …

There once was a king named Jehoshaphat. His name, in Hebrew, means "the Lord judges" and is derived from the same root as Jehovah. He ascended to the throne as king of Judah, the southern realm of the Hebrews, when he was 35. One day, his buddy and in-law Ahab, the king of Israel to the north, talked Jehoshaphat into going to war with him against a local enemy, but Ahab had some serious concerns. A prophet of God had predicted a terrible end of life for Ahab, who had led Israel in worshipping some false gods.

So Ahab connived to trick God.

"You dress like a king," Ahab told Jehoshaphat, "but I'll dress up like a soldier. My costume will fool the Arameans. I'll be safe in my disguise."

The ruse nearly worked. The king of Aram had told his commanders to fight initially with the king of Israel alone. When they saw Jehoshaphat, they figured he was the sought-after target. "Get him!" they shouted.

Justifiably in desperate fear for his life, Jehoshaphat yelled to God for help – and the Arameans mysteriously realized they had the wrong guy. In the process of changing the direction of his chariot, one Aramean commander inadvertently shot an arrow – and it just so happened to land in the opening of Ahab's breast plate, smack in the middle of his chest. The haughty, sinful king of Israel was dead by nightfall.

Jehoshaphat survived. Still, he found himself in a bit of a mess because he had participated in Ahab's attempt to put one over on the God Almighty. "Wrath is upon you from the Lord," a prophet told him. Soon enough, three tribes of nomads prepared to attack Judah.

The impending threat scared Jehoshaphat from crown to sandals. He ordered all of his people to gather in the town square of Jerusalem. They came from throughout Judah. Clearly, the situation was a grave one. Thousands of citizens looked with cautious optimism for strong, decisive leadership, for words that would help them survive the approaching conflict.

Ah, but they didn't witness some stirring address of statesmanship or patriotic challenge from their king. Instead, a trembling, apprehensive king stood in front of the crowd. Instead, they saw him raise his arms toward heaven.

Jehoshaphat prayed.

"Lord, God of our fathers, are you not the God in heaven, and do you not rule over all the kingdoms of the nations? In your hand is power and might, and no one can withstand you. Was it not you, our God, who drove out the inhabitants of this land before your people Israel and gave it forever to the descendants of Abraham, your friend? They have dwelt in it and they built in it a sanctuary to your honor, saying, 'When evil comes upon us, the sword of judgment, or pestilence, or famine, we will stand before this house and before you, for your name is in this house, and we will cry out to you in our affliction, and you will hear and save!'

"And now, see the Ammonites, the Moabites and those of Mount Seir whom you did not allow Israel to invade when they came from the land of Egypt, but instead they passed them and did not destroy them. See how they are repaying us by coming to drive us out of the possession you have given us. O our God, will you not pass judgment on them? We are powerless before this vast multitude that comes against us.

"We are at a loss what to do, hence our eyes are turned toward you."

Boy, oh boy. Could I ever relate to Jehoshaphat!

That's how I felt every morning when I awakened to another day of misery. That was my experience each time I entered the psychiatric floor at the hospital, on every one of my 10 trips to the hospital for ECT treatments, whenever I walked into the medical building for my many trips to the psychiatrist and the therapist. That was my sense when I was unable to work, unable to drive, unable to get out of bed because I couldn't stop crying for hours at a time.

As awful as things got, I had nowhere else to go. My eyes sought after God.

Almost my entire life, I have tried to behave something like the apostle John – by Jesus' side wherever he went. Jesus went to cure Peter's mother-in-law and into the house of a synagogue official to bring a little girl back to life; John was there. Jesus climbed a mountain to chat in his heavenly glory with Moses and Elijah, and he went into a garden to pray the night before his death; John was there. John was among the first apostles called by Jesus and the only one standing at the foot of the cross to watch him die. Good times, bad times, the spaces in between, John was hooked by the love of Jesus Christ and couldn't imagine life without him.

So it was with me. Not that it made me any better than anyone else. It's just who I was. From the moment of my diagnosis with depression, I prayed as I always had prayed. Jesus had been a real presence in my life through high school and college graduations, in my marriage and the parenting of four children. My faith sincerely affected the way I did my work, first for 23 years as a sportswriter and then into a new career of investments and financial advising. And it influenced my free time, which if not spent with my family often was given to prayer and service for my church.

True, I wondered for a while how God could let this ghastly thing happen to me, but I realized it could have been worse and prayed for the disease to pass. Initially, the depression was mild – though more than mildly annoying – as I also tried to deal with moving into a new house and a new career, watching my children grow into feeling they needed me less and then worshiping in a new parish after attending one church for almost 40 years. As mild depression gradually morphed into major depression, all of those changes felt magnified. Life became very difficult. What once had seemed and felt so good, if still less than perfect, now felt impossible.

Somewhere in there, I encountered Jehoshaphat.

I had read the story before and was familiar with the plotline. But never before had his prayer in front of his people so resonated with me. Despite his knuckleheaded mistakes, Jehoshaphat basically

9

had been a good guy. In 2 Chronicles 17, it says, "The Lord was with Jehoshaphat, for he walked in the ways his father had pursued in the beginning." Even when the prophet Jehu rebuked Jehoshaphat two chapters later, Jehu said some good things were found in him because he had been "determined to seek God."

Yet in the face of impending invasion, the humbled king of Judah stood hopeless and despondent in front of thousands of folks who never had seen their flourishing ruler look that way. He had no clue. All he could do was look to God. Not ask. Not beg. Not bargain. Just look.

Seeking God had been my determination before that roaring lion of depression stalked its way into my life. I tried to stay so determined. Reading the prayer of Jehoshaphat, I decided to make it my prayer as well. I rewrote it from what Jehoshaphat prayed in 2 Chronicles 20:6-12 and trimmed it to fit my equally desperate plight:

"Lord, God of our fathers, in your hand is power and might, and nothing can withstand you.

"When evil comes, I will stand before you and cry out in my affliction, and you will hear and save!

"See how this roaring lion is coming at me. Oh God, will you not get rid of it?

"I am powerless against it. I am at a loss what to do, hence my eyes are turned toward you."

I wrote it down, stuck it in my Bible and prayed it every day. *Almost* every day. Sometimes, I couldn't muster the motivation or energy even to open my Bible. On those days, through the flood of tears, I would whisper, "Oh, my God, I'm at a loss what to do, so I'm turning my eyes to you." And I would whisper it again. And again. Over and over.

The worse things got, the more I fixed my gaze on God.

I attended a retreat held at my church, St. Cletus, in April 2005. The "Christ Renews His Parish" weekend was just for men and was meant to energize us to spread the gospel by words and actions. It introduced me to a dozen outstanding men, the brothers I never had. We joined to form a team for the next retreat, for which I was spiritual director. I began to spend an hour a month in personal spiritual direction with a priest. I met to pray and study Scripture weekly with my men's group. I found myself feeling God's presence all day, in all things.

This also was the time of hospital stays and thoughts of suicide, missed work for me and tough times for Donna, the kids and others who cared about us.

I refused to waver in my prayer.

"Oh, my God, I'm at a loss what to do, hence I turn my eyes to you."

What I had forgotten about this whole tale in the Second Book of Chronicles was what happened immediately after Jehoshaphat's public prayer. One day, in the midst of a particularly rough stretch with my depression, I went back to re-read the story, and I didn't stop with verse 12. That's when I found out about a fellow named Jahaziel. He was standing in the crowd that day, minding his own business and probably quite taken by the king's words, when "the spirit of the Lord" overcame him. He started prophesying to Jehoshaphat and the rest of Judah.

"The Lord says to you: 'Do not fear or lose heart at the sight of this vast multitude,'" said Jahaziel, "'for the battle is not yours but God's. Go down against them tomorrow. You will see them coming up by the ascent of Ziz, and you will come upon them at the end of the wadi which opens on the wilderness of Jeruel.

"You will not have to fight in this encounter. Take your places, stand firm, and see how the Lord will be with you to deliver you, Judah and Jerusalem. Do not fear or lose heart. Tomorrow go out, and the Lord will be with you.'"

Need I tell you what happened that next day? Yes, Jehoshaphat kept looking in God's direction. He kept his faith, even though the people of Judah would have to stand perilously close to the enemy for a while. The king told some of the people to sing, others to praise God. And they watched as the three tribes destroyed each other. Not only did the people of Judah survive what once had frightened and threatened them, but they benefited from it. God allowed them to walk into that desert, where the battle had raged, and spend three days taking riches and clothes and cattle from the corpses. As a result, Jehoshaphat found himself celebrating the Lord more joyfully than ever, with an even greater respect and appreciation and closeness with God than he could have imagined before.

All because he recognized his own weakness and the power of God, turned his gaze, and fixed his watch upon the Almighty.

That experience worked for Jehoshaphat. The more I considered it, the more I suspected his experience could work for someone suffering from depression or someone supporting a sufferer of the disease, as well as anyone else who has known deep suffering.

I hoped that perhaps, if I could humbly and faithfully pray along with Jehoshaphat, I also might feel the gentle handiwork of God.

Pray with me, please:

Oh Father God, every day can feel like such a challenge. Talking to you, crying to you, takes all my spirit and energy some of those days. Give me enough strength at least to come before you and lay open my fears and concerns at your feet. And grant me the faith to know you eventually will take them from me.

*** *** *** *** ***

TAKING ACTION: Turn to this section near the back of the book. Find the action points that correspond with this chapter and try to commit yourself to following the suggestions.

CHAPTER TWO:

A DEPRESSED CHRISTIAN?

DON'T MENTION IT

> *"Lord, God of our fathers, in your hand is power and might, and nothing can withstand you. When evil comes, I will stand before you and cry out in my affliction, and you will hear and save!"*

The story is told about a public sinner who was banned from his church. He went to God and grumbled, "They won't let me in, Lord, because I'm a sinner."

"What are you complaining about?" replied God. "They won't let me in, either."

When it comes to mental illness in this country, none of us seems to completely grasp the causes, the ramifications, the treatments. Not those who suffer from the diseases. Not those who love and support the wounded. Not those in the mental health business or the pharmaceutical business, certainly not those in the health insurance industry. Not parents or children or spouses or friends. And not those who sit in the pews at church every Sunday.

Anyone can see a broken leg. They can comprehend triple-bypass surgery or diabetes. A car wreck that puts someone in a wheelchair for life justifiably elicits a surge of sympathy. A baby born with a birth defect reasonably will change the life of a family forever. And if that heart patient or the man suddenly confined to a wheelchair develops depression, well, of course, that makes sense. We all can understand that losing use of your legs or trying to accept that your child never will be "normal" can knock you for a loop.

But only for a while, now. You've got to pick yourself back up and get going with life eventually. You can't spend much time feeling sorry for yourself, having the "blues," letting stress get the best of you. Pull yourself up by the bootstraps, man. Come on, girl, you've still got a lot to live for. You should be happy it's not some really serious disease.

God forbid there's no outward reason for the emotional problem. Heaven help the man, woman, boy or girl who is paralyzed not by a broken spinal cord but by the seemingly inexplicable panic attacks of severe anxiety, or someone who moves from five months of a manic workaholic pace to the depths of suicidal despair because of bi-polar disease. And what of the person who suddenly can't get out of bed for days at a time, inexplicably regards everything in the world from a negative perspective, finds no reason for joy or living?

"Just think positive."

"Get something to eat and you'll feel better."

"Try exercising. That always makes me find the energy I need."

"Yeah, there are a lot of days I feel like being lazy and staying in bed."

"It's all about willpower. If you want to feel better, you can kick the depression."

"Ah, we all get depressed now and then. You'll snap out of it and be as good as new."

All perhaps well-meaning words from people searching for a way to help, but ... wake up, folks! Depression will wreak havoc upon an estimated 20 million to 40 million people in this country this year. Half the people in the United States could experience the disease directly, within their families or their circle of close friends. Medical statistics have estimated that more than 12 percent of all men and almost 20 percent of all women have had a major depressive episode at some point in their lives. Depression and alcoholism, which in many cases is a result of chronic depression because of self-medication, are this nation's two most debilitating diseases. Americans spent more than $10 billion on antidepressants in 2000, a figure that some estimates claim rose to $21 billion by 2007; more than 210 million prescriptions for antidepressants were written as recently as 2003.

Despite that positive influence on the nation's drug stocks, depression affects the workplace and the economy in ways that far outweigh the scales toward the negative. In 2005, the Federal Budget allowed a little more than $1.4 million for the work of the National Institute for Mental Health – an increase of about 23 percent from only four years earlier. The disease creates an enormous drain on the economy, at an annual cost of approximately $150 billion lost directly (because of treatment) and indirectly (because of absent productivity), not to mention inestimable cases of personal bankruptcy. Mentally ill citizens in the United States make up almost 30 percent of the disabled workers in the Social Security Disability Insurance Program, contributing to about $25 billion in government cash benefits as recently as 2001.

In his report to the U.S. Senate proposing the 2005 budget request, NIMH director Dr. Thomas R. Insel said 450 million people worldwide suffer from at least one mental disorder and that mental diseases cause four of every six disabilities in the Western world among workers aged 15 to 44. "By 2020," he said, "psychiatric and neurological conditions will have likely increased their share of the total global burden by almost half, from 10.5 percent to 15 percent."

Insel also noted that 90 percent of the 30,000 annual American suicide deaths are attributable directly to mental illness. That represents more annual deaths in the United States than murder (about 17,000 in 2006, according to the FBI), AIDS (approximately 14,000 in 2006, according to the Centers for Disease Control) and most individual forms of cancer.

Most overwhelmingly, in numbers and consequences that never can be measured, it encroaches on families. The repercussions among spouses, siblings, children and parents are deep and everlasting.

This is a reality our country absolutely must face.

None of this is meant to make other diseases seem comparatively less significant. But only 18 percent of all American adults with depression will receive a diagnosis. Almost half of the undiagnosed still believe they are the cause of their own problems and are living with symptoms that create more and more significant emotional pain.

Yet hospitals, when they seek to cut costs, frequently target mental health first. Insurance companies often won't approve prescribed treatments. Almost three in 10 of those undiagnosed depression victims won't go to a doctor because of inadequate insurance coverage; one major carrier in 2006 unwaveringly would allow just 20 visits in a calendar year per patient for all combined visits to mental health professionals, hardly adequate for someone who needs to see a psychiatrist monthly and psychologist weekly.

Not only does America seem inclined to avoid treating the

problem, it would prefer not even to talk about the disease openly. At least many individuals seem to avoid the subject. The stigma tied to major depression in the 21ˢᵗ century resembles that afforded another disease in previous generations. Remember hearing "the C-word" whispered? "What's wrong with Marilyn?" "Oh, she just found out she has 'the C-word.'" Cancer was "the big C," discussed in hushed tones that led to a quick change of subjects. Patients were so self-conscious about having lost their hair from treatments, missing so much time at work, knowing everyone was speculating on how long they had to live, they turned reclusive. Friends didn't know what to say, so usually they said nothing. Often, friendships and support passed away long before the patients.

Today, ostensibly everyone has been touched by cancer and has turned it into open conversation subject matter. The disease inspires respect, some awe, considerable concern and immediate assistance, but considerably less fear than once upon a time. The stigma has disappeared – in part because even if it hits us, America's pocketbook and attention have decided that cancer will not win.

The Church and her people have embraced that fight. We routinely and openly ask friends to pray for a family member with the disease. Many areas have thriving Peregrine Societies – named after St. Peregrine, the patron saint of cancer victims – to raise money, support and awareness. Schools and community groups routinely advertise upcoming runs or golf tournaments or trivia nights to increase financial and emotional support for breast cancer, testicular cancer, ovarian cancer and all sorts of similarly worded afflictions that caused a previous generation to feel ashamed.

And how do some Christians address depression?

"It is pride, self-centeredness and self-pity that are the root of all depression," writes Malcolm Bowden on his personal website. He has written four books about creation and another, titled "Breakdowns Are Good For You," about what he calls "true biblical counseling." Bowden says someone diagnosed with depression needs to ask himself, "Just how mature a Christian am I?"

Another website's entry, authored by Grantley Morris and professing to trying to help Christians who are suffering from depression, says, "Depression usually marks lost faith in the One with whom I have entrusted my future. It dishonors the One who floods my life with endless love and manipulates for good everything that touches me."

In his book "Spiritual Depression," Dr. Martin Lloyd-Jones wrote that a person suffering from depression and calling himself a Christian is using "a contradiction in terms, and he is a very poor recommendation for the gospel." Elsewhere in his book, Lloyd-Jones said that a depression victim "is still morbidly and sinfully preoccupied with self. ... They appear very humble and full of contrition, but it is a mock modesty, it is a self-concern. ... Forget yourself, leave the judgment to (God); get on with the work."

At www.circleofprayer.com, you will find this from author Mary Mullins: "The rise in depression and suicide rates has become almost pandemic and can, I think, be linked to the drop in belief in God and a prayer life. … We worry and frazzle over things when we should be handing these worries all over to Him."

Jim Enterline has been "ministering to the hurting and addicted" since 1992, according to his Jesus 2 U Ministries website. On that site in 2005, he posted, "I personally believe that the main cause of depression is the direct influence of Satan on our lives. Get yourself into an exciting, on-fire-for-the-Lord church. One in which you can feel God working in the services. Get involved. Get some fellowship, this is where you will get strength to withstand the attack of the enemy. Get into God's Word, study scripture promises and stand on God's Word. Remember … happiness is a choice."

Wow! I didn't know all I had to do was sing loud at my church service and eat donuts afterward, that I could have chosen happiness and thus could have avoided standing in my shower sobbing so hard and for so long that I developed an unbearable migraine – day after day after day.

No wonder people who suffer from depression, especially those among Christian America, are so prone to keep talk about their illness within such a close inner circle. A National Institute for Mental Health study showed that "42 percent of those with a formal diagnosis say they are embarrassed or ashamed by their symptoms, and 16 percent are afraid to talk to their friends." Because of that stigma, they fear the reception they might get from others.

A 1999 study published on the American Medical Association's website defines depressive illnesses as "a group of disorders that occur commonly in the general population" and are "associated with considerable personal suffering, functional impairment and a markedly elevated risk of suicide. ... Only about half of all cases of depression in primary care settings are recognized and diagnosed. Even when cases are recognized, the pharmacologic and psychotherapeutic treatments provided by both generalists and specialists often fall short of standard practice guidelines."

That report went on to state that one of the key barriers in diagnosing and treating depression is related to the stigma attached and made the recommendation that the AMA should work with the National Institute on Mental Health to "increase public awareness about depression to reduce the stigma associated with depression and to increase patient access to quality care."

The stigma clearly remains. Being linked with depression might lose business for a salesman. It might reduce the respect a teacher holds in the eyes of students and parents. Imagine what a congregation might say about a pastor with the disease.

When the media reported that Senator Thomas Eagleton had been treated for depression with electro-convulsive therapy in the 1960s, then-presidential candidate George McGovern dropped Eagleton as his Democratic VP running mate in 1972. He feared voters would shy away from a vice president whose depression had been so profound, and McGovern likely was correct in gauging the reaction of voters albeit incorrect if he expected Eagleton's ability as a statesman was impaired. ECT – referred to by the unholy name of "shock treatments" back then – have advanced considerably in a quarter-century; public perception and regard of the disease, its causes and treatments probably have not.

"Clinically depressed patients cry, 'My God, why hast thou forsaken me?' and sometimes add, 'But I really can't blame you for doing so.' Unworthiness. Forsakenness," wrote John Timmerman in an insightful article in Christianity Today. His wife spent seven weeks in a hospital with post-partum depression and suffered what he called terrifying mental affliction and treatment that included ECT therapy.

Imagine going to bed each night and not being sure which person you will be when you wake up. Will you be so plagued by mysterious grief that you can't get out of bed, maybe for hours? Will you crawl into a ball in the corner of the room, unable to face even your most compassionate of friends? Will you snap with irritation at finding no milk in the fridge? Will you find yourself so paralyzed by unfounded fear that you can't go to lunch with your best friend? Will you find yourself not only unable to tackle the chores on your to-do list but actually lacking the ability to assemble the list?

Will you consider the advice of your spouse, your doctor, your therapist, your spiritual director, your closest friend, your favorite book, and suddenly realize you can't hear your own voice, with your own opinion, speaking in your head? What's more, you can't even find a way to distinguish the guidance of God among all those voices.

Will you wish that for an hour, much less a day or so, you could take a vacation from yourself? Will you find yourself so exhausted just inhaling and exhaling that your growing desire is to stop?

And will you feel guilty about all of that because well-meaning Christians tell you that all you need is to believe and trust, to have a stronger faith?

In "The Catholic Encyclopedia," it says that while some suicides are attributable to mental illness and various forms of depression, the Church rejects the "false philosophy" of doctors, moralists and jurists that suicide always is the result of mental disease. The Church "considers that those unfortunates who, impelled by despair or anger, attempt to take their life often act through malice or culpable cowardice. In fact, despair and anger are not as a general thing movements of the soul, which it is impossible to resist, especially if one does not neglect the helps offered by religion, confidence in God, belief in the immortality of the soul and in a future life of rewards and punishments."

Raymond Lloyd Richmond, Ph.D., is involved with the website www.chastitysf.com and has been published in "Catholic Psychology" in association with his "A Guide to Psychology and its Practice." He regards a lack of trust as the root of all anxiety and a lack of trust in God's justice as the root of depression. "Of course," writes Richmond, "just like Saint Paul, all those who live devout Christian lives will experience periods of uncertainty and anguish – all aspects of personal suffering. Just look at the lives of the saints. But if everything is accepted with complete faith, none of it has to become a psychiatric disorder."

Later in his writing, Richmond acknowledges that psychiatric medication "can be useful in some extreme cases – such as schizophrenic, bi-polar disorder and severe episodes of major depression – but for the most part, the use of psychiatric medication primarily supports the secular scientific error that you can 'feel better' without having to alter your lifestyle to assume moral responsibility for your life."

Some of his suggestions for curing depression include:

- Think of Christ on the cross, hated and despised, and the role that played in being resurrected with him.

- Read what St. John of Avila had to say about St. Paul's suffering and faith, and what St. Rose of Lima wrote about grace and tribulation.

- Download a Catholic relaxation recording to your MP3 player.

- Study the basics of true faith with a cover-to-cover reading of the "Catechism of the Catholic Church" and the Bible.

- Remind yourself you are worthless and deserve nothing but condemnation without Christ, yet in Christ are offered forgiveness.

Let's put aside, for a moment, the enormous challenge for a depression victim to tackle even a part of those tasks. It is dubious whether any or all of them would actually prove medicinal or curative for an extended period of time before the victim would run into failure to live up to the requirements to continue such a regimen, and failure is tantamount to a death sentence to someone suffering from major depression.

Two more of his suggestions truly stand out beyond any of those others. He said:

- "If you have a lack of interest in usually enjoyable things, then rejoice, for your Christian mission in life is not to enjoy yourself but to proclaim the Gospel of all times by making constant sacrifices for the salvation of other souls."

- "If you have thoughts of death, remember that only by dying to this world can we be born to everlasting life, and that until God alone decides our time here is finished we must devote all our energy to hard work in his service. So be honest with yourself and recognize suicide is just a way of saying to God,

'My will – not Thy will – be done.'"

I believed, with all my heart, the first part of Jehoshaphat's prayer: *"Lord, God of our fathers, in your hand is power and might, and nothing can withstand you. When evil comes, I will stand before you and cry out in affliction, and you will hear and save!"*

That's the way I was raised. I had accepted Jesus as my savior, the Lord of my life. I knew where to turn in time of distress.

I accept as true much of what these writers say – at least pieces of it, taken with an attitude of compassion and grasp of the reality of situations. But it is incredibly naïve and ignorant to tell depression victims that they feel alone, desperate, hopeless, even suicidal because they are supposed to make sacrifices as a Christian or because their belief in God is phony and not good enough. The Catechism and the Bible are wonderful, life-changing books, with holy opportunity to meet God, and the lessons to be learned from the lives of the saints can be important.

The problem is that if a sufferer doesn't have the energy to get a glass of juice out of the refrigerator in the morning or pick up a telephone to call a friend in a moment of dire need, how can he or she be expected to extensively read a book – or even open that book?

John Timmerman's wife, Pat, in a brief journal entry during her depression, confided, "I feel so guilty that I can't seem to get well. I feel like a stranger to myself. ... I can't read my Bible or pray. I know

God knows my needs and the needs of my family, and I trust He will take care of us all. I've reread my favorite Bible promises. But I can't feel them right now."

Some bouts of depression probably have evil origins. No argument here. Carrying the burden of sin or addiction can bury a Christian under an intolerable yoke. Satan plays a role at times, in moments when prayer or reception of the sacraments or reliance on faith in Christ can prove victorious.

In April 2005, I was scheduled to make that retreat at my parish with more than a dozen other men. I had been looking forward to the weekend for months. Yet at the hour I was supposed to leave the house, I thought there was no way I could do it. Depression turned into severe anxiety, an acute panic attack. I laid on the couch, then face down on the bed, paralyzed with fear of walking out of the bedroom. Donna helplessly felt that if I didn't find the motivation and strength to make the retreat, the depression would have won a major battle in the war and it could prove decisive. When she said something about that moment being the work of the devil, something stirred inside me. My faith forced open my heart just long enough for the muscle of Jesus to lift me and carry me to that retreat – where I met a group of brothers in Christ who became vital in my personal skirmishes during the ensuing months. Satan had known that. He had chosen a key moment to muster all his forces against me and nearly prevailed.

One day's triumph didn't end the campaign. The depression didn't disappear that day. The problems in my brain – how my body processes serotonin and norepinephrine and whatever other physical reasons reputedly instigate the severest forms of the disease – didn't go away by force of my will or strength of my faith. Major or severe depression might be the result of factors out of a person's control. For instance, it can be linked to genetics. Large and extended depressive episodes can be caused by traumatic events such as death of a child or loss of a job. Or the depression can develop gradually over time, for reasons that aren't easily pinpointed or for that matter possibly discerned at all.

What does make obvious sense is that giving a victim orders bigger than he or she can manage only sets them up for failure. Telling them their inadequate faith has created the situation, been the cause for all the heartache and concern and disruption among family and friends, only adds to guilt and makes a horrifying state of affairs worse.

Is it any wonder, then, that so many people with depression not only fail to turn more fervently to God but falter in their beliefs and relationship with their Lord, even lose their faith entirely? They speculate why God would put them through such an ordeal, allow so much pain. They shout to him in anger. They pray for help, guidance, a light to show the way and arms to carry them. When they don't see any of that materialize quickly, in an obvious way, they surrender to the foe.

All the while, well-meaning fellow Christians blithely and blindly quote James from his Epistle, to "consider it all joy when you encounter various trials, for you know that the testing of your faith produces perseverance."

A little understanding – one of the gifts of the Holy Spirit, by the way – could go a long way in providing the encouragement and support the victim needs during the trial.

That was the first step Jehoshaphat took in his prayer. He understood the reality of the situation, how serious and desperate things were. And then he recognized what God had always been during the good times of life, what he and his forefathers had vowed to do if difficulty ever appeared in life. He acknowledged that God is more powerful than any situation. He praised God. Jehoshaphat ordered his people to fast, helping to focus all their heart, mind and body on the Lord, and then drew attention to all of God's might to the point of cherishing the role God had granted the Jewish people throughout history.

He allowed God two key roles in his life: listener and savior.

Yes, Jehoshaphat had an army and the throne. He could have summoned the nation's every resource, called for help from neighboring peoples and attacked the enemy before the enemy attacked first. That's what most rulers would have done. That might have been what the nation's citizens expected.

Forget what conventional wisdom might have suggested as the proper decision in that moment. Jehoshaphat, a king, humbled himself in front of his people and witnessed that he needed help out of the situation.

And Jehoshaphat conceded he wanted a friend to be there with him.

Pray with me, please:

Lord, God of our fathers, in your hand is power and might, and nothing can withstand you. When evil comes, I will stand before you and cry out in my affliction, and you will hear and save!

Help me to recognize you in the midst of all that seems confusing, disturbing, frightening. I need to hear your voice, or at least simply know you are near, when I am surrounded by darkness. And please, help me not to be discouraged when I am unable to follow some of the well-meaning yet impossible advice of those around me.

***   ***   ***   ***   ***

TAKING ACTION: Turn to this section near the back of the book. Find the action points that correspond with this chapter and try to commit yourself to following the suggestions.

CHAPTER THREE:

REST STOP – BEAUTY IN THE CLOUDS

The man planned to rise at 6 o'clock in the morning. To anyone who knew him well, that didn't happen often. He wasn't a "morning person," so a 6 a.m. wakeup call signified some incredibly special motivation.

This was an extraordinary idea. Looking at the world from a bluff on the west bank of the mighty Mississippi River, rising early would give him a chance to see the sun ascend over the Illinois farm fields. Before he came to spend the weekend here at this retreat house, several men told him the view of the sunrise would be one of the highlights of the stay, one of those true recognitions of the glory of God in nature, a moment to freeze in the memory and inspire prayer for the rest of his life.

But when he awoke that first day, he knew instantly he wouldn't see a sunrise. The sky was filled with clouds. Rumblings from the distance foretold an imminent thunderstorm. So it was back to bed, covers pulled to his chin for another hour before the call to morning prayer.

I'll just see it tomorrow, he supposed.

The next day, a Sunday, his body woke on its own at 5:30 in the morning. He listened. Already the thunder had returned, and soon enough he could hear the rain pounding the sidewalk just outside his window. A half-hour later, at that 6 o'clock moment when his alarm was supposed to signal the presence of beauty, he peered out the shades for the view across the river. He barely could see the enormous river, certainly didn't have the much-anticipated artwork of God's sunrise achievement to admire in quiet worship. Only another heavy storm, thunder rolling sometimes for more than a minute, huge raindrops, lightning splitting the sky sideways.

Just another dose of disappointment. Usually a man would enjoy an extra, unexpected hour of snoozing early on a Sunday morning. Not him. He couldn't sleep, only listen to the rain and thunder and lament what wasn't there – what he felt he was entitled to experience.

Later, when the rain had ceased, he strolled along the walkway atop the bluff and inadvertently turned his gaze to the Eastern sky. There, a bank of clouds appeared high above, the wide puffs stacked one upon the other like a huge gray-silver-black-white stairway to heaven. He found himself mesmerized.

And he recognized: storms can be as beautiful, as necessary, as awesome as a sunrise. The grass and trees seemed greener than they had the day before. And those trees were alive with the songs of dozens of birds. The air smelled fresh, clean, filled only with the sweetness of hundreds of flowers that just had taken a long drink to satisfy a powerful thirst.

Somewhere on one of those plains to the east, a farmer who had worried over his drought-wracked pastures danced in the rain out in his front yard. A little boy walked toward his church and stomped in a puddle on the parking lot, as he delighted in soaking his good Sunday shoes and laughing at the rainwater filling his mouth. A woman grabbed her camera and dashed outside to capture a flash of lightning. A couple glanced at the day lilies on the back porch and felt grateful the flowers would lose that droopiness they had displayed.

On the western bluff overlooking the river, the retreat's morning prayer was about to begin. The sun would shine before day's end. Life would feel normal, bright, the same as it usually did. Maybe even better than expected for those who could recall the early hours of the day.

How he wished he had kept his eyes open during the storm.

Pray with me, please:

Sometimes, the hardest thing to say is thank you. Even when I don't feel grateful for anything, give me the strength to say, "Thank you anyway, God."

***   ***   ***   ***   ***

TAKING ACTION: Turn to this section near the back of the book. Find the action points that correspond with this chapter and try to commit yourself to following the suggestions.

CHAPTER FOUR:

"OH GOD, WILL YOU NOT GET RID OF IT?"

"See how this roaring lion is coming at me.

Oh God, will you not get rid of it?"

Found on AmericanCatholic.org: "*Certain Catholic saints are associated with certain life situations. These patron saints intercede to God for us. We can take our special needs to them and know they will listen to our prayers, and pray to God with us.*"

Consider, again, the patron saint of cancer victims.

St. Peregrine had cancer of the foot so severely that he was scheduled for amputation. During prayer the night before the surgery, Peregrine had a vision of Christ appearing before him and touching his foot. The next day, his foot was cancer-free — for good. An inspiring saint from whom we can request prayers of intercession for friends and family stricken with cancer.

Thank God for St. Peregrine.

Meanwhile, there is no true patron saint of depression. Yes, the Old Testament character Job is a patron for the disease, but what depression victim could compare his personal plight to that of perhaps the least fortunate man in human history and find a truly kindred soul?

There are several patron saints of mental illness. Among them is Bibiana, who refused being forced into prostitution and so was put into a "madhouse." And Christina the Astonishing, who had epilepsy and was thought either holy or insane. Saint Drogo's mom died during his birth, so he grew to practice extreme penance out of guilt. The most recognized patroness of mental illness is Saint Dymphna, whose mother died when she was a teenager. Soon, her king-father made sexual advances on Dymphna, who refused and was killed by her dad as punishment.

Surely there has been a saintly or blessed man or woman, presently by the side of Christ in heaven, who lived a life normal in most ways save for an extremely impressive devotion of faith and a period of suffering from depression.

To be sure, the disease has plagued many well-known figures even in relatively recent history.

Abraham Lincoln was a long-time depression victim. Joshua Wolf Shenk has written a book about it: "Lincoln's Melancholy: How

Depression Challenged a President and Fueled His Greatness." In an October 2005 Atlantic Monthly article on the subject, Shenk wrote that "Robert Wilson, who was elected to the Illinois state legislature with Lincoln in 1836, found him amiable and fun-loving. But one day, Lincoln told him something surprising. Lincoln said 'that although he appeared to enjoy life rapturously, still he was the victim of terrible melancholy,' Wilson recalled. ... 'When by himself, he told me that he was so overcome with mental depression that he never dare carry a knife in his pocket.'" Indeed, Lincoln admitted to considering suicide often.

"A tendency to melancholy," he once wrote a friend, "let it be observed, is a misfortune, not a fault." To another friend he wrote: "I am now the most miserable man living. If what I feel were equally distributed to the whole human family, there would not be one cheerful face on the earth. Whether I shall ever be better I can not tell; I awfully forebode I shall not. To remain as I am is impossible; I must die or be better, it appears to me."

Albert Einstein had the disease. So did Theodore Roosevelt and Winston Churchill, who called his depression "the Black Dog."

Saint Francis of Assisi suffered from depression. In his book "The Journey and The Dream," about St. Francis, Murray Bodo wrote about the day "when (St. Francis) had risen from his long illness and staggered about the green hills and found that they no longer lifted his heart. He was only 22 years old then. It had been a bright day ... but their beauty had only depressed him. The heavy spirit of melancholy had him in her grip, and he didn't understand, didn't want to understand why. ... If only (the townspeople) had known the emptiness and despair he suffered."

That's right: God-fearing, saintly people have lived with the roaring lion, set to devour them. Recall Job's troubles. He was considered blameless and upright, feared God and avoided evil. A series of events turned his world upside-down – oxen stolen, herdsmen killed, sheep and shepherds struck down by lightning, camels pilfered and the camel herdsmen killed, all his children slaughtered by a great wind. He suffered boils all over his body and scraped at them among ashes.

"Perish the day on which I was born," Job cried, "the night when they said, 'The child is a boy!' May that day be darkness; let not God above call for it, nor light shine upon it. ... I have no peace, nor ease; I have no rest, for trouble comes!"

Early in Genesis 15, Abraham certainly seems to be suffering when he laments to God his childless state. Jonah's anger with God over the conversion of Ninevah sent him into a fit of depression in Jonah 4: "Now, Lord, please take my life from me; for it is better for me to die than to live." When a large gourd that had provided Jonah shade in the searing hot sun died, he again turned despondent and asked for death.

In the 20th chapter of Jeremiah, the prophet had to undergo the embarrassment of being placed in stocks and a public scourging. It plunged him into the depths of a depressive episode, as he chastised God: "You duped me, O Lord, and I let myself be duped; you were too strong for me, and you triumphed. All the day I am an object of laughter, everyone mocks me." He would try to sing praises to God, try to recognize God as the eventual champion over his persecutors, but at last he cried, "Why did I come forth from the womb, to see sorrow and pain, to end my days in shame?"

In the 88th Psalm, King David sang these emotions: "You have put me in the depths of the pit, in the regions dark and deep. Your wrath lies heavy upon me, and you overwhelm me with all your waves."

And again from David:

"I am wearied with sighing;

All night long tears drench my bed;

My couch is soaked with weeping.

My eyes are dimmed with sorrow,

Worn out because of all my foes."

Psalm 6:7-8

The Psalms are filled with such pitiable woe and distress. David endured sorrow so deep and despair so wide that he couldn't feel God's presence on many occasions. He doubted, speculated if God might have abandoned him permanently. Would anyone have dared tell

43

David to just snap out of it? And how to question the faith of God's other best friends in the Old Testament?

Ready for this? Even Jesus experienced bouts of depression. Logic says so, for one thing. We are taught that Jesus, the Word incarnated into flesh, experienced every temptation, sadness and joy known to man.

Wrote John Timmerman: "Jesus, the true light himself, the very son of God, stands in the form of humanity – the very same who marred God's perfection and cast darkness over that light. To restore that light, Jesus, the perfect light, underwent the full anguish of complete darkness. He knew separation from God thoroughly; he plumbed the deepest sea of terrifying darkness in order to build a bridge out of it for us."

Our Lord wept when moved by the grieving Mary over the death of Lazarus, her brother and his friend. He wept when he saw the city of Jerusalem, as he grieved that the people there would not accept the peace he preached. At one point in the Gospel of John, many of Jesus' disciples left him because they couldn't come to grips with his teachings. Things had proved too difficult for them. His support group dwindled, and the human side of Jesus' nature probably wanted to be liked, accepted, sustained when the going got rough. Some of those departed disciples might have been special friends. Jesus turned to his twelve apostles and asked, "Do you also want to leave?" You can sense the distress in that question.

Surely he felt a bit distressed when he was rejected in Nazareth, his hometown, the place where he had gone to school and worked as a carpenter, laughed and played and made friends. When his cousin John the Baptist was murdered. When he knew how many people wanted him dead as well. When he realized how many lepers and others needed his healing touch, wanted a piece of him, and there simply wasn't enough time in the day. When his right-hand man Judas betrayed him. When his choice of a leader, Peter, wouldn't even admit knowing him. When he felt "sorrow and distress" in the Garden.

Oh, Jesus knew times of depression. Science has proven that it is possible for a man to sweat blood during moments of extreme anxiety, something Christ experienced while praying in the Garden of Gethsemane. "My God, my God, why have you forsaken me?" -- Jesus prayed that on the cross, cried that, suffered that feeling of despair along with so many of us.

On John McMan's website entitled "When Your Brain Goes Crash," he posted the thoughts of some Christian depression sufferers. Andrea, who was a recovered alcoholic for 15 years, wrote that she is a very spiritual person but "when down, I don't go to Church, pray or meditate as much." Erica's husband is miserable in trying to support her through her difficult times; he hasn't divorced her because they are Christian but tells her she "should just get a grip."

45

On Sept. 25, 2003, someone called Eaglepoint posted this: "The voices that call to me each day. ... Today will be the day I find peace in the next life, but at the end of the day I still find myself in this vale of tears. Crying to God to please take me home. I see friends pass and envy them. I want death so bad but what stops me from doing it myself is how will God see what I've done. I feel trapped, damned if I do, damned if I don't."

Jesus actually provided a means of determining whether a person suffering from depression is dealing more with issues of sin and evil than with a natural human affliction that perhaps has its roots in deeply physical, mental and emotional problems.

In the Gospel of Luke, Jesus said to his disciples, "A good tree does not bear rotten fruit, nor does a rotten tree bear good fruit. For every tree is known by its fruit. ... A good person out of the store of goodness in his heart produces good."

Early in the throes of my depression, I examined the "fruit of my tree." I have done it several times since then. The work I have done – the work the Lord has done through me – has been good. As a father and husband, as a writer and active member of my church, as a retreat leader and investment advisor and friend, I genuinely have tried to be a dedicated man of prayer seeking to walk in Christ's footsteps.

Yet in the late fall of 2001, I couldn't get out of my recliner for hours at a time.

I would sit in that recliner and tell myself, "In five minutes, you'll stand up and get to what you need to do." Then it was in 10 minutes, then a half-hour. That's how it began, how the roaring lion sat crouching in wait, stalked, hunted, then commenced slowly to devour me from the inside.

See how it comes after me. God, can't you stop it?

The baseball season had ended. A sportswriter at the time for the largest newspaper in Missouri, I had spent most of September shadowing the San Francisco Giants and Barry Bonds as he pursued, then broke Mark McGwire's home-run record. October was spent writing about the baseball playoffs and World Series, then McGwire's retirement from the St. Louis Cardinals. I had plenty of comp time accumulated from working almost every day since the previous February, so many winter days I didn't need to work much at all. Not that it had mattered to me in years past. A workaholic, I always found a way into the newspaper – or a magazine, or a book. Or I would dive into parish council activity at church. Or watch and coach my kids in sports. There always was something.

Late that fall and into the winter, something subtly changed. I would stay in bed later than usual, plop in front of the TV and not move until it was time to pick up my kids from school. Donna was at work, my boss didn't need me most days, so I was left entirely to myself for hours. I wasn't sleeping well at night, so I felt tired all the time. I had little appetite. I often didn't want to be around people – not co-workers, family or friends. I rarely smiled or laughed. I grew irritable at times. Mostly, I was quiet.

Convinced something out of the ordinary was happening, I visited our family doctor, who diagnosed depression. He prescribed a low dosage of one of the more common anti-depressant medications, and both of us assumed my mood would improve in time for the Cardinals' spring-training camp in February.

Instead, life deteriorated. I would feel glued to my chair for hours, frozen by an extremely and highly unusual low ebb of energy, no motivation even to change out of the clothes I had slept in or to shower. My self-esteem, which always had been healthy, plunged into a pit of absolute failure. Often, tears would come for no discernable reason. I bellowed angrily and sharply at my wife and kids at times, shut myself off emotionally and physically from them at other times. I felt such despair involving the state of things at the newspaper where I worked that I quit the job I had held for almost 18 years – my dream job, gone. I had what seemed sensible reasons for the change, but I really didn't give it the thought and attention and dialogue I should have.

I rarely missed Mass on Sundays and still was heavily involved in parish activities, but I felt unhappy with many aspects of that church and my priest, an apathy that I felt was prevalent there. Indeed, when I did miss Mass on occasion, that's when Donna knew something serious was at work. Even though I was able to focus on the necessary study of my new career as an investment representative, it didn't fill up all the time in my day and didn't satisfy the emptiness that was developing where once my positive self-image had thrived.

I stayed in prayer and Scripture, as I spent considerable time with the Psalms and the Gospel of Matthew. Many days, I had energy only for prayer, and not always extensive prayer at that. Sometimes, just barely enough to get started.

Soon, I realized the problem was bigger, deeper, more complicated than my family doctor could treat. I began to visit a psychiatrist, but my depression turned out to be a frustrating challenge for him as well. Name an anti-depressant in the family of drugs that treat serotonin deficiency and I have taken it – Paxil, Prozac, Lexapro, Wellbutrin, Zoloft, Celexa, Effexor, Cymbalta. I've tried the tricyclics – amitriptyline, imipramine and nortriptyline. Eventually, I also tried the monamine oxidase inhibitor EmSam (a new drug in patch form) as well as older drugs Parnate and Nardil.

Complicating matters were a persistent migraine headache, which I had combatted for 30 years but found growing worse, and sleep problems. Many times, I would endure stretches of getting no more than a total of seven hours of sleep in three consecutive nights, when the anxiety would take deep root. So my doctor had me working on that as well, with everything from Ambien to Xanax.

All the while, I was visiting a therapist anywhere from once a week to once every few weeks, depending on how well things were going and what insurance allowed. I switched from one therapist to another in search of a comfort zone. Talk therapy, I found, is a gradual process. Eventually, we went to work on cognitive therapy techniques, which entailed my scribbling down any negative thoughts, identifying the specific category into which the thought fit and rewriting the thought in a positive manner. The theory was to make that a habit, to the point that I naturally could convert those destructive thoughts into something dispassionate or harmless. It worked -- somewhat.

*   *   *

"Be gracious to me, LORD, for I am in distress; with grief my eyes are wasted, my soul and body spent. My life is worn out with sorrow, my years by sighing. My strength fails in affliction; my bones are consumed."
-- Psalm 31:10-11

*   *   *

Some of the drugs succeeded, albeit insufficiently. I had bad physical reactions to some. Others proved completely ineffective. Finding the right combination was more than elusive, as it apparently is for about 30-60 percent of all depression victims. For me, it seemed impossible.

And the bad days persisted.

Hindsight reveals no such thing as a "worst day," since everything measured equally dreadful for myself and my family. It is possible to put the most difficult days into three periods: major depressive episodes, electro-convulsive therapy and suicidal.

Unfortunately, I don't remember a lot of details about all of them. Depression has a way of infiltrating the memory banks, wiping out some things entirely while merely scraping away at others. It's one of the more nagging aspects of the disease, especially for me. I always had a lockdown memory, often for the most trivial of things. My kids used to delight in playing a game in which they would name a year, any year since the late 1800s, and I would spout something that happened historically significant in big-league baseball. Those memories don't drop into my mind as quickly now.

Worse than that, I don't remember much from Christmas 2005, less than two months before my first ECT treatment. I was the spiritual director on a retreat in October that year. By mid-February, after I had undergone a couple treatments, I only remembered having been present at the retreat and not much more.

It had been the worst major-depressive episodes that made Donna and me decide to follow my doctor's advice to undergo the treatments. The roaring lion was voraciously gnawing at me on an almost-daily basis. I wouldn't sleep any more than three or four hours a night, though often less than that. It would take me several hours to fall asleep, that despite trying nearly every sleep medication on the market. I would lay in bed for hours, staring and praying, fearing what kind of life was ahead for someone like me and despairing that I wouldn't be able to make enough money to support my family or be the husband Donna needed or the father my children needed. I would nod off for a while, then awaken as the thoughts, the fears, the dread all returned and kept me from sleeping again for two or three more hours.

That turned the next day into an unpredictable ride. I often felt as though I had a hangover all day as I tried to do my work. I could get the basics of my job done well most of the time. I checked the quality of investment portfolios and stock performances. I called clients to see if they had any needs or suggested changes to them. If I had a meeting with a client, I could focus for that hour and perform as well as ever. But I didn't make nearly as many phone calls as usual, didn't make contact with enough prospective clients to build my business up to the expectations I had set. Anxiety gripped me every time I prepared to pick up the phone to call someone I didn't know well – and that was so unlike me that I didn't recognize myself.

Imagine starting each morning inside a cave, with thousands of people outside hating you and doing all they could to get inside at you. A huge boulder rested inside, large enough to cover the opening of the cave but close enough that it could be rolled to block the way and thus preventing the enemies from entering. So each day, your first effort was to push and strain in attempt to roll that thousand-pound rock to a place where you felt protected and expected to get on with the business of living and loving, able to get on with something close to normal. Most days, before any damage was inflicted by the invaders, you succeeded in blocking the entrance. You sighed with relief.

Then, it hit you: You are inside a cave. Alone.

You realized you were too exhausted to do anything else. What's more, not only had you shut out the enemy, you had shut out your friends and family, who didn't understand how to come inside with you, and you hadn't known how to explain the essential role they could play for you inside that cave.

Imagine doing that every single day, and looking ahead unable to perceive an end to the practice. Nothing really accomplished other than living.

The end of almost every day left me feeling more and more like a failure.

Those were the good days.

* * *

"As the deer longs for streams of water, so my soul longs for you, O God. My being thirsts for God, the living God. When can I go and see the face of God? My tears have been my food day and night, as they ask daily, "Where is your God?"" -- Psalm 42:2-4

* * *

I awoke every morning with two thoughts. First: "Damn, I woke up." I didn't want to wake up. I wanted to die. I wanted to be finished with it all. The exhaustion, the frustration, the absolute work involved just in taking a breath and existing was too much.

If my primary care doctor had called and said, "We just found you have a brain tumor. You have only a few days to live," I would have felt relieved. Grateful that I could disappear without any of the guilt involved in taking my own life.

No thought seemed logical, yet I couldn't stop thinking the worst about myself. "You are a horrible dad. Your kids deserve so much better than you. They're getting older, going off to college, and they don't need you. They don't love you like they did when you could be a real dad to them, back when they were little. Donna should have more than you in a husband. She deserves someone who can be there for her, someone who can listen to her and hold her and be affectionate with her, support her, be her partner. You can't do that. She'll realize pretty soon that she doesn't love you any more. You aren't going to be able to pay your bills. There's no way you will get enough new clients to earn your keep. The company is going to give up on you eventually. Your friends – Jean, Larry, Brian, Mike – your parents, Donna's parents, your sisters, they don't understand how hard this is for you. Sure, they are trying now and they are supportive now. But they'll wear out. You'll see. You are a horrible friend. Face it, man, you're just a miserable human being."

I lamented the years when my children were little. Even though I had been around a great deal, I wished I had been around all the time and mourned for those years. I missed my old job, the people there whom I no longer saw, and my heart was torn with grief. I suffered over things large and small, financial and emotional and spiritual. I wondered how God could love me, why Jesus accepted the agony of the nails for me.

Satan talking? You bet, in the voice of my depression. But it wasn't just about evil. I prayed constantly, surrendered myself each day, tried faithfully to attend Mass and prayer gatherings. My friend Larry had given me a gold cross embedded with the "Medal of St. Benedict," on the back of which were initials standing for the Latin prayer of exorcism against Satan. The English translation, which I began to pray daily, is: "Be gone Satan! Never tempt me with your vanities! What you offer me is evil. Drink the poison yourself!"

* * *

> *"LORD, my God, I call out by day; at night, I cry aloud in your presence. Let my prayer come before you; incline your ear to my cry. For my soul is filled with troubles; my life draws near to Sheol. I am reckoned with those who go down to the pit; I am weak, without strength. My couch is among the dead, with the slain who lie in the grave. You remember them no more; they are cut off from your care. You plunged me into the bottom of the pit, into the darkness of the abyss. Your wrath lies heavy upon me; all your waves crash over me." -- Psalm 88:2-8*

* * *

My second daily wakeup thought: "Damn, I've got to live like this for another day."

Sometimes, I started crying before leaving bed. Other times, the tears didn't begin until I was in the shower. They always came eventually, and never were they merely a mild aggravation. They could keep me in bed for hours. I would sob, heaving, moaning in loud and deep agony such that my entire body seemed to participate in the pain. The result would be a migraine so severe I couldn't turn my head suddenly left or right without feeling it would burst. The tears sometimes would stop long enough for me to walk downstairs to the couch, where I would sit and watch hours of TV, not really enjoying it or paying attention to it yet unable to go anywhere, unmotivated and completely void of liveliness and barely clinging to life.

Then, there were times when no tears were able to flow. The sadness was every bit as deep and acute, but I couldn't cry. I felt numb, dulled to being able to transfer the feeling into some visible outlet that would relieve the ever-intensifying pressure that built within. The tension multiplied but felt incarcerated, as though the feelings had been some culprit and not allowed the freedom of seeing the light of day.

Once the ECT treatments began, I had no choice. All of me became imprisoned. I underwent 10 of them, covering a little more than three weeks. Donna would drive me to the hospital early each Monday, Wednesday and Friday morning. She would sit in a small waiting room, where relatives of other patients slowly would appear as well. I went into a room to lie on a table and begin the process of preparation, strapped to a table and electrodes attached to my head, for just a few seconds of electricity zapped into my brain. My memory is limited to that table and a couple of the people who worked there. Every other memory is completely absent. For about six weeks, I wasn't allowed to drive. I couldn't work for two months.

Unfortunately, like the many medications I had tried, electro-convulsive therapy didn't cure my depression. That doesn't mean it didn't help. Before the ECT my anxiety was manifested in panic attacks so severe that my hands would tremble visibly, my chest would feel like something heavy was sitting on it, and I couldn't imagine being around groups of people, even the closest of friends and family. After the ECT those attacks disappeared entirely for a time, later returning but at not nearly as acute a degree. And it allowed some of the drugs to work well enough that I could concentrate – a little better, at least most of the time. It enabled me to begin making progress doing some of the things my psychologist wanted – slowly, most of the time.

But I never could say I felt good, not during the two months I was on leave from my job after the ECT and not in the ensuing months. I came to feel that the depression was simply a part of me, that I had to accept it as a piece of who I was.

* * *

"Listen, God, to my prayer; do not hide from my pleading; hear me and give answer. I rock with grief; I groan at the uproar of the enemy, the clamor of the wicked. They heap trouble upon me, savagely accuse me. My heart pounds within me; death's terrors fall upon me."
-- Psalm 55:2-5

* * *

Author Andrew Solomon, who suffered from depression and wrote about it in "The Noonday Demon," related living with the disease to a story about returning to some woods in which he had played as a child. There, he "saw an oak, a hundred years dignified, in whose shade

I used to play with my brother.

"In twenty years, a huge vine had attached itself to this confident tree and had nearly smothered it. It was hard to say where the tree left off and the vine began. The vine had twisted itself so entirely around the scaffolding of tree branches that its leaves seemed from a distance to be the leaves of the tree; only up close could you see how few living oak branches were left, and how a few desperate little budding sticks of oak stuck like a row of thumbs up the massive trunk, their leaves continuing to photosynthesize in the ignorant way of mechanical biology."

People looking at me from a distance might not have sensed anything was wrong. When I returned to work after undergoing ECT, I was able to handle the basic demands of the job almost every day. Some of my clients knew I had been on medical leave, but once I assured them I was back in the saddle, all was well. If someone had known about my depression but weren't privy to what happened behind the closed doors of our home or my prayer meetings or the confessional or my office, they might have thought I was headed back to good health.

The good news really was that most days, I awoke without wishing I was dead as my first thought – or even a thought at all. My first thought about twice every five days was to say my morning prayer. Prayer became as important to me as eating; my conversation with God, time spent just resting in his presence, actually kept me breathing most days.

So most days weren't bad days. But there were no good days.

I still could begin crying for no apparent reason, tears that wouldn't stop. I looked at life happenings such as my daughter Erin's graduation from high school and impending move three hours away to begin her collegiate years as something akin to having my right arm chopped off. If my son, normally not given to calling frequently or chatting for no necessary reason, would be quiet or spend a lot of time at friends' houses, I assumed I had failed him as a father and he didn't want to be around me. Youngest daughter Kara graduated from eighth grade and moved into high school, which meant my days of coaching her and that group of girls on the basketball court were in the past, a loss that created a great deal of heartache. I missed spending that time with her and thought we never could be as close as we had been. I would argue with my oldest daughter and knew, I just knew, that I had neglected all the things I should have done to be the right kind of dad for her, that any mistakes she made were my fault.

As someone who relied on commissions for most of my paycheck, I would look ahead two months on the calendar, not know for certain what business would come in and fly into a panic; I figured I was rotten at my job and a terrible provider for my family.

And even though Donna not only stuck by me but propped me up with a positive, supportive, incredible love, I thought for certain the day would come when she would want a complete husband and leave me.

* * *

"LORD, hear my prayer; let my cry come to you. Do not hide your face from me now that I am in distress. Turn your ear to me; when I call, answer me quickly. For my days vanish like smoke; my bones burn away as in a furnace. I am withered, dried up like grass, too wasted to eat my food. From my loud groaning I become just skin and bones. I am like a desert owl, like an owl among the ruins. I lie awake and moan, like a lone sparrow on the roof." -- Psalm 102:2-8

* * *

Andrew Solomon wrote that at a certain point, "I would have been happy to die the most painful death, though I was too dumbly lethargic even to conceptualize suicide. Every second of being alive hurt me."

Not all depression is the same; not all victims are the same. Unlike Solomon, I did "conceptualize suicide." The idea hung around like a ne'er-do-well acquaintance. It made me nervous, afraid sometimes, but I didn't run from it. I sat down with it, listened to it, examined it out of curiosity. Looking back, I'm not completely certain what kept me from embracing the idea of taking my life out of resignation if nothing else.

Actually, I do know what prevented me from trying the idea

on for size: My Lord and God, through the love of my family and friends.

The first time I knew that the thought actually was a threat came in June 2005. Donna and our two middle children were spending the week at a retreat; Jessica, our oldest, worked a great deal and spent most of her free time with friends. Kara was the only other person home one particular night when my depression went to work at its hardest. I had an almost-full bottle of sleeping pills and another of anti-depressants; the sleeping pills hadn't ever helped me sleep but I knew they could have a lethal effect if taken in volume, especially if added to other powerful pills.

The bottles stood on top of my clock radio, on the night table next to my side of the bed. I lay down and stared at the pills – all night. I would cry some, blink away the tears, feel them streaked on my face, hurt all over my body. I never slept. I prayed some, spent a great deal of time quietly wondering ...

But the next day dawned with me still alive for one primary reason: I was haunted by the vision of my youngest daughter being the person who would have come in, shaking me in hopes of waking me up, unable to do so. God saved my life through the presence of my Kara, my deep love for my daughter.

I shared that "close call" with my doctor, my wife and some trusted friends. Naturally, they were frightened by the possibilities, not just the one that had passed but those to come. Donna and my friend Jean, in particular, made me promise to call for help if such a night ever came again. I vowed I never would leave Donna that way. I promised Jean that I wouldn't let her down. I envisioned the kind of life my children would have to live with the fact of their father having committed suicide, and I pledged to myself they wouldn't have to feel that reality.

So when my mind filled with thoughts of suicide again in late July that year, when I knew I didn't have enough strength within me and that for a night my faith couldn't overcome the misfiring that was happening in my brain, I called my psychiatrist and checked myself into the hospital.

After having experienced that once, I knew how horrid the psychiatric ward could be. It would have to take a powerful bout with depression to make me consider spending even one night there, and it would be a sign of strong love for my family and friends – and myself – to make the call to return there.

I made that call in May 2006. I went back to the psych floor because I knew I wasn't safe by myself on the outside.

I returned by the grace of God, not because I didn't have a faith strong enough to withstand the situation. He gave me the strength to make the call to my doctor when I was too weak to survive on my own. He gave me a great and unconditional love through my family and friends to motivate me to want to hang on to life when everything in my head tempted me otherwise. He was by my side when I jumped into a pit of darkness, when I trusted Him to jump with me and be there with me in that pit.

And yet, in the summer of 2007, when I thought perhaps I had reached a place where I felt able to manage a life with depression as a companion, I found myself back on the sixth floor. I had ingested a handful of assorted pills I had been hoarding for some time. There could have been only one reason for collecting those pills. I kept telling myself I was doing better, when all the while my depressive side was making plans that came to fruition. I took the mixture of medicines late on a Friday afternoon. Donna and I went to dinner with another couple, and I had a large glass of my favorite red wine – and kept extending my glass for more each time the waiter went by.

The next thing I remember, it was Saturday morning and I was in a hospital bed; I began crying uncontrollably. I begged God to let me go home, yet I avoided talking at length with God. I felt so horribly embarrassed.

I had failed again. Failed to ask for help in such a desperate moment.

And failed, as well, to end it all.

* * *

"LORD, hear my prayer; in your faithfulness listen to my pleading; answer me in your justice. Do not enter into judgment with your servant; before you no living being can be just. The enemy has pursued me; he has crushed my life to the ground. He has left me in darkness like those long dead. My spirit is faint within me; my heart is dismayed."
-- Psalm 143:1-4

*   *   *

Through all those months, the pain had come at me from every angle. There had been emotional and mental anguish. Although I never lost my faith, there had been suffering of the spirit as well.

And the pain involved the social side of life. Many, many times I didn't feel like being around friends and often avoided what phone calls came from them. I fibbed about how I was doing when some people asked because I knew they didn't really understand, so there was no point in including them in the truth of my existence. Yet I internalized when people didn't call to find out where I was or what I was doing or how I was doing. Every day, I wrestled with that strange, illogical paradox of not reaching out for support from some old friends but feeling a bitter wound caused by those silent, out-of-touch friends.

And I experienced severe physical pain, from headaches and a general, non-specific throbbing in my limbs to constant bowel problems and a routine hangover-like effect from never getting even half a good night of sleep.

"I had thought that when you feel your worst your tears flood, but the very worst pain is the arid pain of total violation that comes after the tears are all used up, the pain that stops up every space through which you once metered the world, or the world, you. This is the presence of major depression. ...

"With the depression, your vision narrows and begins to close down; it is like trying to watch TV through terrible static, where you can sort of see the picture but not really; where you cannot ever see people's faces, except almost if there is a close-up; where nothing has edges. The air seems thick and resistant, as though it were full of mushed-up bread. Becoming depressed is like going blind, the darkness at first gradual, then encompassing; it is like going deaf, hearing less and less until a terrible silence is all around you, until you cannot make any sound of your own to penetrate the quiet.

"It is like feeling your clothing slowly turning into wood on your body, a stiffness in the elbows and the knees progressing to a terrible weight and an isolating immobility that will atrophy you and in time destroy you."

from "The Noonday Demon"

In answer to all those critics who express an opinion that a depression victim actually is overly selfish, there really is nothing selfish about depression. A selfish person wants only what is best for himself, expects the entire world to cater to his needs. Life is a matter of ego, stinginess, a concern with his personal welfare alone because he arrogantly assumes his self to outrank everyone else.

Alas, the reality of depression creates an animal something on the extreme opposite end of the spectrum. People with the illness actually would like to help someone else more than they can describe.

In my experience, I sought excuses to reach out to others more than usual, to ask about their lives and listen to their stories more than usual. If I was able to help with homework, cook dinner for the family, listen to a friend's problems, provide some insight to the others at my prayer group – if I had the strength to get started on any of those relatively minor projects or opportunities to help someone else, I wanted nothing more. Those tasks, which under other circumstances would have seemed insignificant or trivial, proved magnificent in that they told me I had at least a little value, some purpose.

Yet depression victims do find themselves overwhelmingly *self-absorbed.*

Someone suffering from depression has such a low perception of his value that he doesn't think he is worth anyone going to the trouble to do something for him.

No matter what he is doing, he can't stop thinking about what is happening with himself, can't forget for a day or an hour or a minute that he has the illness, if only because of the effort he has to summon to take the next breath and the next step. It lingers in the shadows of his mind sometimes, not in the open consciousness. No matter how well things are going that day, the reminder of his depression floats like background music.

He hears it. Trying not to is futile. The more he aspires to shut out that constantly noisy tune, the more he finds himself humming along and soon drawn entirely into the orchestration.

Solomon wrote in an essay entitled "Anatomy of Melancholy:"

"When you are depressed, the past and future are absorbed entirely by the present, as in the world of a 3-year-old. You can neither remember feeling better nor imagine that you will feel better. ... Depression means that you have no point of view."

The siren song of depression always is there. Fearsome. Alarming. Formidable.

Lurking like a lion, hunkered down at times, prowling other times. Always ready to bare its teeth and devour its victim.

That was Jehoshaphat's great concern, what drove him to his knees in front of the subjects of his kingdom. His messengers had warned him that three armies of enemies were fast approaching. Jehoshaphat had no quick answer, no physical answer at all that inspired any confidence or trust. He saw danger headed his way, like a train bearing down the tracks – and Jehoshaphat felt tied down tightly, inescapably.

His vast riches and weapons couldn't stop the train. His people, his family, his friends lacked the strength or influence to jump on and apply the brakes. But the train was coming so fast, and it was so big, and it looked so dangerous. Stopping the train might not have been enough; he wanted it derailed and sent someplace else far, far away.

He loved and respected God. So did his people. Surely God would stop the massacre.

Pray with me, please:

See how this roaring lion is coming at me. Oh God, will you not get rid of it? I can't help but feel the pain, Lord, or remember so clearly how much I hurt. Surely there must be a way out. I would surrender myself to that way, commit myself to that road. I can't see it, though. Show me that way.

***   ***   ***   ***   ***

TAKING ACTION: Turn to this section near the back of the book. Find the action points that correspond with this chapter and try to commit yourself to following the suggestions.

CHAPTER FIVE:

REST STOP – NEIGHBORHOOD PRAYER

A full moon shined brightly as I began my walk through the neighborhood one evening in early September. So bright, actually, that I didn't even look up and take notice. The moon apparently reflected so much of the sun's light, from the other side of the world, that it gave the appearance of dusk when in reality it was more than an hour past sunset.

As I stepped out of our driveway, took a right turn and headed up the street, I could see the hallmark lines of a lawn mowed earlier in the day. The smell of fresh-cut grass was wonderful and stayed with me for several strides.

Thoughts of friends who are ready to adopt two baby boys from Guatemala came to mind, and I prayed for them -- until I noticed where I was.

My walk had brought me to the end of the first block. A look to my right showed a house – clearly illuminated – owned by an elderly woman I know. A sweet lady. Her husband died, what, two years ago now? I know she's lonely, still misses him every day. God, please comfort her. A look to my left – good people, really good people, live in that two-story. Their daughter died of cancer almost 30 years ago. Seems like yesterday. It must hurt sometimes for them to see her friends from high school marry and have kids, now to watch *those* kids graduate into college years. She never reached graduation age. Lord, please ease that pain when they miss her.

I stepped across the street. Another prayer for another widow. And the family over in that house really has had a difficult time the last few years. God, could you …

Wait. It seemed darker all of a sudden.

I looked up. The moon was partially hidden by some black clouds, with a large wall of even blacker ones approaching. Rain? A storm building? I couldn't tell. But my eyes kept watching the sky. I tried not to change my leisurely pace, wanted to look at the homes and think of the neighbors who lived there, to notice for-sale signs and barking dogs and the aroma of flower gardens. But the status of encroaching clouds and obscured moon proved magnetic.

I watched as the dazzling white dish in the sky was covered entirely, though the clouds couldn't hide all its light, some slipping out through a break – a small hole in the heavens. As the whole sky, it seemed, moved right to left, the completely full moon filled that hole and my walking world felt stunning and alluring once more.

Just that quickly, as quickly as the thought came, the moonlight disappeared. Completely. Only blackness filled the sky, east to west and north to south. Not even a glimmer of light snuck through.

I still could see to walk, thanks to streetlights and porchlights and the headlights of an occasional passing car. I hardly noticed. My head tilted back, my eyes could not leave where the moon had hung. It's still there, isn't it? Behind the clouds? Still full? Still bright? The clouds will pass, right? I looked. No end in sight. God, the moon can't just go away like that – forever. What kind of sky is that, swallowing our moon, a moon there just for me this night?

How am I going to make it through the rest of my walk?

My pace changed. I moved even slower.

Moon! my mind screamed. Come back!

At last, I reached my driveway again. The house seemed aglow. Every light must have been turned on. Inside, safely inside, were my wife and family, probably folding laundry and watching TV, talking on the phone and laughing.

I sat on a lawnchair on the back porch and looked up – still only blackness – then closed my eyes. My hair and clothes still were dry; the storm, if it came now, wouldn't touch me. Without realizing it, I whispered, "Thank you, God." And in my heart, I could hear, "God is love. God is love. God is love …"

I stayed silent and listened.

"God is. God is. God is."

Some time passed. I didn't know how long. I simply sat there.

"Is. Is. Is ..."

Before I ever opened my eyes, I knew. I could feel the glow with all my body. I slowly open my eyes. I looked up.

That night, at that moment, it might have been the brightest full moon I have ever seen.

Pray with me, please:

Jesus, my brother and friend, I know instinctively that you walk with me, take every step by my side. Help me to trust that instinct you have planted in me. When all around me is darkness, may I feel your light of love, of compassion. Increase my faith.

***   ***   ***   ***   ***

TAKING ACTION: Turn to this section near the back of the book. Find the action points that correspond with this chapter and try to commit yourself to following the suggestions.

CHAPTER SIX:

"I AM POWERLESS AGAINST IT"

When our son, Josh, was a baby, he developed some serious digestive problems and didn't sleep through the night for the first eight months of his life. That created a couple of zombies for parents. I was working long hours. Donna was spending the day tending to him as well as Jessica, our toddler daughter. Our batteries never got recharged with a good night's slumber.

One particular night, we heard him crying in his bassinette in our bedroom. I probably was only half-awake when I climbed out of bed, walked over and picked him up. Right away, I started walking the carpet up and down one side of the room. Assuming he needed to burp after eating, I jostled him gently, sang, hummed, tenderly tried to coax him to stop crying and go back to sleep.

Donna lay in the bed with her eyes only partially open at first. Both of us had gotten used to him not going back to sleep. We were frustrated and worn out.

Slowly, Donna began to wake up. The realization finally struck her. "Mike," she asked. "Did I *feed* him yet?" We were trying to think of everything we could to help him sleep, something we thought would be good for him and us. But in the midst of our exhaustion and trying so hard to help with all sorts of ideas, we had neglected the obvious and most basic need of the moment. The boy needed to eat.

When you are powerless, the key answer to your most pressing problem can be extremely basic.

Recall the story of the prophet Elijah. In the First Book of Kings, the queen Jezebel sent a messenger to Elijah telling him, basically, that she had a hit list with one name on it: his. Knowing that if he stuck around town another day, he would be dead, Elijah fled by himself into the desert.

"He came to a broom tree and sat beneath it. He prayed for death: 'This is enough, O Lord! Take my life, for I am no better than my fathers.' He lay down and fell asleep under the broom tree." (1 Kings 19:4-5a)

Getting away from all other people. Praying for death. Sleeping with no hope for improvement in a distressing situation and unable to summon the energy or motivation to solve the problems or seek any help.

Yes, Elijah was a classic victim of depression.

God didn't grant Elijah's wish, of course. Nor did he erase

Elijah's depression or the despair. He didn't send another messenger from Jezebel telling Elijah that all was safe at home, either.

No doctor cured the sickness. No friends appeared with any magical pick-me-up words.

Yet God cared.

"Then, an angel touched him and ordered him to get up and eat. He looked and there at his head was a hearth cake and a jug of water. After he ate and drank, he lay down again, but the angel of the Lord came back a second time, touched him and ordered, 'Get up and eat, else the journey will be too long for you?' He got up, ate and drank; then strengthened by that food, he walked forty days and forty nights to the mountain of God, Horeb. There, he came to a cave, where he took shelter." (1 Kings 19:5b-9a)

God sent Elijah the basics. Food. Water. A clear sign of his presence and love in Elijah's life. Not complete strength, but strength enough to get through.

Like Jehoshaphat in his own dire situation, a victim of major depression actually is powerless initially. No matter how much you try to force yourself into the life you once had, returning to the person you once were, that simply cannot happen. No matter how much others around you tell you to get back on the horse, you don't have the ability to ride such a horse at this time in your life unless you want to feel like the worst cowboy in the rodeo and you don't mind spending just a few seconds in the saddle before finding yourself tossed into the air and landing hard on the ground over and over and over again.

Don't feel guilty about that powerless feeling. Acknowledge it. Whether you are the CEO of a major corporation, a stay-at-home mom used to "having it all together" in the midst of chaos, an investment representative, a college student or whatever your job or calling in life, keep in mind that suffering is part of being human. This is the type of suffering you have to endure right now.

Granted, it's not good for the old self-esteem. But ...

Who are you afraid of letting down? Or try the question this way: Who are you trying to please?

Your spouse? Your kids? Your boss or clients or co-workers? The standards of "a good life" set by the world? Yourself? I've got news for you: As much as your family loves you and as much as your ego needs the approval of others and as much as you need the job, none of those matter as the most important component in life. When you die, you can't take your job or your new car or your big house or your friends or even your family with you. It's just you.

And God.

Yep, just you and God. And God knows you are powerless against this roaring lion. He *made* you, don't forget, so he made all your weaknesses and flaws and powerless nature. God knows not to expect perfection out of you in life. In fact, because he most clearly understands all your weaknesses, God probably expects less of you based on your own doings than you do.

God is waiting for you to discover Him in your weakness. He might not have created the depression; that might just be one of those inexplicable things that happens in life. But he *is* there *in* the depression. He has the power to help you get through it, even to emerge from it.

Before discussing all the things he has sent to help you, know this: Don't look for God to come down from the heavens with some amazing cure. That's not to say that can't happen. Jesus told us that whatever we request in prayer with faith, God will grant. The Father might not grant a cure, though, or at least not as quickly as we would wish and perhaps not in the way we would want or expect.

Elijah didn't necessarily get what he wanted. God provided what he needed, both at that moment and for the journey that followed.

God gave Elijah the basics -- sustenance, a reminder that He was there, some direction. God has provided you with the same resources.

*   *   *   *   *

FIND HELP FOR THE CHEMICAL PROBLEM

First and foremost, know that if your depression has been diagnosed as "major," there is some kind of chemical problem in your brain. So make sure you are seeing a psychiatrist regularly. Not just any psychiatrist. Find a doctor who clearly cares about you and your depression, who listens and responds, who makes you feel comfortable and confident in his efforts on your behalf.

Sometimes I feel like my doctor expects and wants to cure my depression more than I do. Once, I told him that I felt OK most days, that I could get into the office almost every morning and attend Mass every Sunday, eat enough to stay basically healthy and tend to the chores around the house. I had accepted that the depression probably was just a part of my being, same as someone with diabetes or high blood pressure has to make a similar acceptance. The disease might get in the way at times, perhaps flare up to the point of making life miserable for a while, but that was better than some of the alternatives.

"That's not acceptable," my doctor responded. "No one should have to live like that. I want to keep trying until we find something that works completely."

God has given medical science an opportunity to create medications that can help those of us with depression and has filled the medical profession with caring men and women who truly want to end your suffering. Allow yourself to accept those gifts.

* * * * *

TALK TO A PROFESSIONAL TALKER

Meet regularly with a psychologist. Again, not just any psychologist. It is vital to find a therapist with whom you connect. Personalities are vital in the patient-therapist relationship.

The first therapist I saw seemed like a good woman with all the right intentions; she also only took patients on Saturdays and occasionally answered her cellphone when it rang with a problem involving her other job. I didn't feel important to her. So, in essence, I fired her and tried someone else.

Something clicked this time. I immediately felt comfortable, that I was understood and accepted. And I felt she cared about me. When I had a reaction to some medication one Friday and my psychiatrist was on vacation, I received what I thought was poor advice from one of his colleagues; my reaction worsened to the point that I was having a 24-hour anxiety attack of extreme proportions. I called my therapist. She talked with me long enough to help me understand it probably was a reaction to the new drug and not anything about me, nothing that I had caused, and eased some of the guilt I had begun to feel. What's more, she was truly empathetic with my situation; I could hear the concern in her voice.

She immediately will remember the names of my wife and children, along with their approximate ages, where they go to school; the name of my best friend, what my relationships are like with the important people in my life, the value of my faith, all without any reminders from me. And she never has tried to solve my problem completely or cure my illness, never has said I will be rid of the depression if I just keep a journal or start exercising and eating right immediately. She patiently, slowly has helped me progress. And she has challenged me often, not allowed me to wallow in self-pity or lack of effort.

Don't fall under the illusion that talking with a caring friend is enough. Your friend can't be as objective and in some cases knows too much of your history. Find an unbiased person who will care but doesn't have to tiptoe around whether she should say certain things or avoid delving into certain subjects.

Talk therapy in many cases is more effective in treating major depression than medication; the most effective treatment probably is a combination of both. If you aren't meeting with a psychologist you trust and believe in, find one immediately.

* * * * *

LET YOUR FAMILY LOVE YOU

Consider the people you want to see on Christmas Day each year -- your spouse, your children, your parents, your siblings, perhaps your grandparents if they still are around. There is a reason God has created a family for everyone at birth. We need other people, people who love us and want to support us. Don't be afraid to lean on them

or call on them for help during your suffering. You would do the same for them, right?

Well, OK, for some depression victims perhaps their family is one of the root causes. There might be personality differences. Maybe your spouse or parents don't really understand that you have an illness that can't be defeated by sheer will. Perhaps you want to spare your children the heartache of seeing their mother or father in tears and looking like a complete wreck. You might not be talking with some members of your family. Or maybe you don't have much family at all, with children grown, parents and spouse passed away.

If you are reading this, though, you likely have some member of your family -- close or extended -- who loves you. Who worries about you. Who wants to help you through any difficulty. Whom, if the situation was reversed, you would want to help. If you truly lack a family member willing to help, you can create your own family unit by joining some type of community and finding yourself surrounded by caring people.

When they offer a ride to the doctor's office or want to bring dinner one night, allow them to do it. If your husband or wife offers to cook breakfast or pack a lunch to help you eat better, or to take a walk with you in the evening, say yes. If all that your children want is a hug and a kind word, some sign that you still love them, show them in whatever small way you have the strength to do.

They won't heal you. That's all right. All they really want to do is love you. Let them.

* * * * *

LET YOUR FRIENDS LOVE YOU

You may have a job with co-workers you have gotten to know well. You may regularly attend a church where you participated in a few activities through the years. You have friends.

Yes, no matter what you say, you have friends. A neighbor you chat with now and then. Someone you have had fun with, laughed with, maybe cried with in the past, be it recent or much longer ago. God gave all those people to you. Again, accept the gift. Consider them extended family, though in many cases they might know more and understand more about your disease than your family does, they might care more about you and respond more genuinely to your needs than your family can. Look around. Keep your eyes and ears open. Notice how many times people truly have wanted to help you.

The help can be so simple. The group of men in my prayer group at St. Cletus knew of my depression and had heard some of the tales about the depth of suffering. When I began my ECT treatments, they got organized and took turns bringing dinner to our house one night a week. Normally, I would have felt too proud to allow someone to do that, but I realized they were responding out of love.

Many of those men, including some to whom I am closest, acknowledge they don't understand my depression, but they haven't judged. They have simply cared. When I saw them after Mass on a Sunday and they asked how I was doing, I didn't have to answer with a superficial "I'm just fine" if I really wasn't; I could tell them if it had been a rough week, felt their compassion and knew they would pray more fervently for me and my family.

At the same time, it can be equally as important to limit your time spent with some well-meaning people who drain your energies. You have to stay focused on what is best for your health.

* * * * *

SPEND TIME WITH GOD

Recognize that God and a relationship with him are the most important, most nourishing, most strengthening, most basic elements of your life.

Find a prayer group at church, whether a Bible study or just folks like yourself who want to pray together, and join it. You don't have to become the most active member or even speak up very often. But God wants us to be a part of a community of people -- the Body of Christ, His Church -- and bond together in prayer.

Away from a prayer group, in times when you are alone, pray then as well. Set a time every day, maybe even for just a few minutes at first. Treat it like an appointment with your doctor and use that time to talk with your God. If all you can do is recite a few prayers you learned as a kid, then do it. If all you can do is say, "Please, God. Thank you, God," even if you don't know what to ask for and don't feel particularly thankful, do it. Make yourself do it.

And find a spiritual director. This might not be something that would come to mind readily and might not happen easily, yet it is more important than you realize. The person could be the priest or minister from your church, or the leader of your prayer group, or perhaps someone from a ministry that exists for the sole purpose of providing spiritual direction or companionship or consolation. Someone who will listen as you bare your soul.

Like finding the right psychiatrist or psychologist, the first spiritual director you choose might not be the man or woman you feel best meets your needs. You want to sense the person is there to care but not cure, to listen and understand without judging, to help you find the way God is leading you and not be that guide himself. But just as God sent all those other people to help take care of your chemical, emotional, psychological and mental needs as you deal with the depression, don't underestimate the need for help dealing with the spiritual aspect.

The spiritual director I saw when my initial need was the greatest was a priest who was at St. Cletus when we began attending that church. He had plenty of knowledge about depression as a disease but spent more time listening to me talk about my relationship with God, how I prayed and why, how my spirituality affected my relationships with others and my vision of myself. He would suggest a book I could read at times, help me explore some ideas or goals other times. Mainly, he allowed me to open my soul to the words of my relationship with God.

When all is said and done, God has sent you so many angels loaded with provisions for your long journey through the desert of depression. It's up to you to assemble them all together into something of a loose-knit team, with each member as important as the others.

Take note that even with the touch of an angel and nourishment sent from God, Elijah still found himself walking through the desert, a wasteland of scorching heat and loneliness. A land of depression, where a man's heart either seeks God or abandons belief altogether.

Emerging from the desert, Elijah hid. "Why are you here?" God asked him.

Life wasn't immediately good again.

"I have been most zealous for the Lord, the God of hosts, but the Israelites have forsaken your covenant, torn down your altars, and put your prophets to the sword. I alone am left, and they seek to take my life." (1 Kings 19:10)

Consider that to be Elijah's farewell speech – or so he suspected.

He had fled all people, his job, his home. He was alone in the desert. No one could understand his plight; he had no ability to turn things around. His best friend could have walked into the cave and told him to get home, get to work, face his problems. His neighbor could have listened to Elijah's problems and told him about some real trouble the guy on the next block was facing, that Elijah could handle Jezebel. There would have been no convincing Elijah. He was finished. Done. See ya, God. I did my best. But I can't get out of this, I just can't do it. And you don't seem prone to curing me, God, so that's it.

Once more, God didn't wave his hand and "make it all better." Not right away. And not in the manner Elijah would have preferred.

God actually seemed to say that since he had Elijah's full attention, he would teach him something important.

"Then the Lord said, 'Go outside and stand on the mountain before the Lord; the Lord will be passing by.' A strong and heavy wind was rending the mountains and crushing rocks before the Lord – but the Lord was not in the wind. After the wind there was an earthquake – but the Lord was not in the earthquake. After the earthquake there was fire – but the Lord was not in the fire.

"After the fire, there was a tiny whispering sound. When he heard this, Elijah hid his face in his cloak and went and stood at the entrance to the cave." (1 Kings 19:11-13a)

No great sign of God's power, though Almighty God could

have been in the wind or the earthquake or the fire if he had wanted to be. Instead, he wanted to make sure Elijah was paying rapt attention to him, that he drew so close as a whisper, an intimacy set aside only for the most cherished of friends. Whispers are reserved for secrets between best friends, for flattery between lovers, for warmth between parent and child.

God wanted Elijah to know that no matter how desperate his world seemed, he loved Elijah and would not leave his side.

Elijah still lamented his plight, repeating his despair to God. This time, God told Elijah to go home and there he would anoint Jehu as a new king of Israel and Elisha as his successor prophet. In other words, he told Elijah that he would give Elijah friends to help him fight his battle. Godly friends, people who would not necessarily understand all that Elijah had experienced in the desert but who would be there for him.

Again, God provided basic human needs – unconditional love from God and unconditional love and support from fellow humans.

You've probably heard it said that "God helps those who help themselves." Bad advice. Don't believe a word of it. If you are out to help yourself, you want to be in control. You want to have the power and might over your life and job and family. You want to be God.

God wants you to know that feeling of no control. Again, the depression likely isn't a creation in the Father's master plan, but God does want you to experience what it's like to be weak and in need. That's where He will meet you.

As we have seen, that's also where Jehoshaphat found himself. He decided there was no shame in telling and in showing the entire world that he was powerless against what was rushing toward him. He was a king, but feeble. He was incredibly wealthy, but defenseless. He had the support of an entire nation, but lacked the ability to maintain its survival.

Jehoshaphat put aside his arrogant pride.

Arrogance. That's often the greatest sin we commit as victims of depression. We look back at a lifetime of fighting our own battles. We started our own business, or worked our way up the ladder, or raised our children with little help from anyone else. We're Americans, and we don't look for help from anyone else. Tell us the odds are stacked against us, and that simply inspires us to work harder than ever. It's about winning. There's room for only one man or woman on the victory stand.

Self-actualization says we each have the ability to do anything we want. Empower us, and we can handle anything the world sends our way.

Alcoholism? Addiction to cigarettes? Over-eating? I can stop whenever I want. Getting into better shape with a diet or exercise program? I'll start when I'm ready, and then you will see how great I'll look.

Depression is the same. Or that's what we're told. Each man or woman has the tools inside to think positively enough and summon the motivation to emerge from the funk. Right?

Jehoshaphat taught us otherwise. He bowed to God in humility and admitted his weakness. That was all God wanted to hear.

Pray with me, please:

Good and gracious God, grant me the gift of humility. Allow me the grace of feeling the depression's presence. Enable me to stop seeking the strength in myself alone. God, I truly am powerless against this enemy. And that's OK – because I know you have the answers. I'm listening, Lord.

***　　***　　***　　***　　***

TAKING ACTION: Turn to this section near the back of the book. Find the action points that correspond with this chapter and try to commit yourself to following the suggestions.

CHAPTER SEVEN:

REST STOP – LIFE CAN HAPPEN BENEATH THE SURFACE

As someone who worked every day on a face-to-face basis with investors for more than five years, I became closely familiar with many men and women among the retired population of this country. I loved getting to know them, which meant hearing the stories about their grandkids, their flowers, their golf games, their health and their charitable activities.

I really enjoyed listening to tales of their vacations. Many retired folks today have the money, the time and the dreams to travel all over the world. So I lived vicariously through them as they regaled me with stories about walking the streets of Rome and the Holy Land, cruising the Caribbean and seeing the colorful autumn foliage in New England.

After a while, I noticed an interesting trend that I know

continues. More and more people are taking summer vacations to Alaska. They are attracted by the kind of beauty no one can see or describe anywhere else in the United States, the untouched landscape, the slow pace of life in so many simple, small towns that remind them of a day gone by.

I never fail to ask questions and learn something new about the places people go, and I find myself particularly fascinated by Alaska.

One client told me about something especially interesting: The largest of all the North American squirrels is native to Alaska.

(OK, so I amuse easily …)

Honestly, it's called the Arctic Ground Squirrel, known as the tsik-tsik to the local Inupiat Eskimos because of a sound the animal makes when threatened or distressed. This squirrel lives on the arctic, alpine tundra and is found most specifically in the ice-free mountainous regions of the Denali National Park, about 150 miles southwest of Fairbanks.

The tsik-tsik has an unusual life, to say the least, certainly not typical of any other squirrel and vastly unlike every other mammal in the world. It doubles its body weight during the summer by consuming far beyond what would seem natural or healthy. Then, in July, it begins insulating its burrow with various grasses and eventually, after crawling inside, blocks the entrance with dirt.

The fat little tsik-tsik then digs as far as three feet into the earth in preparation for a winter that will witness temperatures above the ground reaching as low as 40 degrees below zero. The animal wads itself into a tightly wound ball and, with the ground around it falling at times to zero, tsik-tsik somehow – still baffling scientists – reduces its body temperature from 98.6 degrees to 26.4 degrees, the lowest known to any mammal. Every once in a while, the creature shakes just a little, enough to raise its body temp to about 70 degrees, but only for a while and exactly what it does during that time remains a mystery.

The squirrel remains far beneath the surface of the earth, void of contact with any other tsik-tsiks or sunlight, not to mention hungry predators and the bitter, deadly cold for more than half the year.

These little creatures enthrall scientists. The squirrel's extensive time in constant darkness does something to the molecules in its body, which switches its fuel consumption from glucose to fat along with the reduction in temperature.

The combination of curious factors could have positive effects some day for those of us in the human race. Researchers think studying the squirrel could help in fighting obesity and type-2 diabetes. Some scientists are studying things from a completely different angle, as they wonder if it might lead to a breakthrough that would enable long-distance space travel or keeping internal organs viable for transplant for longer periods of time.

Bio-chemists find themselves asking questions such as:

- When does the body know it's time to switch from burning glucose to fat?

- What actually sets off hibernation?

- How can the balance of exposure to light and darkness help cure depression?

One scientist has observed that the tsik-tsik digs so deep, escapes light and life so completely for so long, perhaps something about its new form of existing – a new way of learning how to live, if you will – might have something to do with exactly that new reality. The tsik-tsik spends six months in utter, complete, impenetrable darkness. Maybe darkness is a classroom, if not actually the teacher.

In some tests done on mice, a specific kind of gene was turned on by darkness. That pitch-blackness, where the normal way of seeing and knowing are useless, signaled an opportunity to do something different, to express itself in a new and positive way. And it couldn't be just a few moments of darkness or even a few hours. Scientists noted that the mouse needed to be plunged into unqualified darkness for at least 48 hours – which to a wild mouse probably feels like an eternity.

Said one scientist: "We asked, What is the common environmental factor faced by hibernating mammals? I can only think of one consistent environmental factor, and that is constant darkness."

In the book "The Hibernation Response," the authors pointed

out that cavemen dealt with the cold, depressing winter by moving deep into caves or burrows, where they gathered in huddles to share body heat. Their metabolism fell to extremely low levels. Frankly, they slept away the worst times of their lives.

As we have evolved, man has dismissed that instinct to hibernate. The book's authors say that we have become "walking hibernators."

Anyone who has suffered from depression – "walking hibernator" seems like a fitting term – can relate to the tsik-tsik. Depression victims know what it's like not to want to see other people, leave the house, perform the routine of what seems like a normal life – and certainly fear that many things "above the surface" are either predators or simply wouldn't understand their way of life.

It's not just a desire to burrow into the harsh environment of bitter cold and pure blackness; it's a necessity, something out of the victim's control, an obligation and compulsion that emanates from some mysterious place within.

So maybe depression has a purpose after all. Maybe men and women find themselves pushed deep within themselves, into their complete darkness, in order to find a new way to live, learn lessons about survival that can't be discovered in other ways.

As a result, we can emerge leaner, smarter people with a perspective those who never have spent time in the darkness can't understand.

Pray with me, please:

Dear Father, all you provide is good for me. That includes the darkness. Adjust my eyes and my heart so that even though I'm not able to see clearly in the surrounding blackness, I trust that something fine will emerge in me. All I need do is trust. Please, God, give me the grace to trust.

***   ***   ***   ***   ***

TAKING ACTION: Turn to this section near the back of the book. Find the action points that correspond with this chapter and try to commit yourself to following the suggestions.

CHAPTER EIGHT:

"I AM AT A LOSS WHAT TO DO"

The most memorable days in the life of a parent are those when their children are born. Granted, I haven't experienced a wedding involving any one of my four kids. But it's hard to imagine anything more emotional and festive as the days I first met each face-to-face.

I celebrated the birth days of each in a similar way: I went home from the hospital, put on Amy Grant's "Age To Age" album and played the tune "Sing Your Praise To The Lord" as loud as my stereo's speakers would allow. Then I would whirl around and sing -- probably off-key, but it didn't matter.

I was a daddy. Nothing could have lifted me higher into the clouds.

That said, those first hours after I became a father on June 15, 1985, didn't inspire a feeling of awe as much as it scared my socks off.

Our daughter Jessica was born that day – 2:14 p.m., DePaul Hospital in St. Louis County. She was our first child. Donna had gone into labor but, as we expected, had to undergo a Caesarean section because she was too petite to give birth naturally. So I was allowed to hold Jessica before Donna had the opportunity. The nurse put her into my arms almost immediately. That was only the second time in my entire life I had held a baby. The first time came when someone thrust my new cousin into my lap about 11 years earlier; completely mystified on how or what to do, I quickly gave the cousin back to my aunt.

I couldn't give Jessica back. She was mine. I had to take care of her.

And I couldn't have been more clueless.

I'll never forget the first time she, um, well, the first time she dirtied her diapers. Donna couldn't just hop out of bed to deal with it, since she was fresh from surgery. She looked at me. "Well, Dad," she said. "Have at it." Have at what? I actually asked if we could buzz the nurse. Nope. This was a job for a parent. A dad. I buzzed the nurse anyway.

I looked down at the squirming, pink little creature and knew she needed me. But I literally had no idea how to meet her needs, not even the smallest and most basic of human requirements of this completely dependent child who had no other choice but to cry to me for aid. And then, when I finally figured out how to undo the diaper and opened up the package – have you seen what comes out of babies that first day? I thought she was defective. Humans aren't supposed to produce such sticky, pitch-black tar like that. How was I supposed to clean it off her bottom? How was I supposed to put on a new diaper? How was I supposed to be a father to this little girl, to help guide her through the hills and valleys of life when I never had given thought to it for even a moment?

I was at a complete loss what to do, how to begin, where to turn.

Jehoshaphat knew that feeling. And he wasn't ashamed to admit it, before God and all his people. He faced an approaching enemy, certainly much more imposing than a little newborn. After acknowledging that he was powerless to deal with the enemy, he humbled himself even further. Jehoshaphat divulged that he didn't know what to do.

Should he grab a sword and fight until what likely would be his inevitable death?

Should he scream obscenities at the onrushing horde? Maybe the foe would roll around in unceasing laughter long enough for Jehoshaphat to come up with a real plan.

Should he turn tail and run?

Oh, how tempting and how easy it might be simply to call it quits. Even if it's not a matter of suicide, it could be crawling into bed each morning, rolling up into a ball and refusing to face the reality of the disease within and the world without. Alas, choosing to live with the disease of depression often might seem the most difficult choice. Philosopher Soren Kierkegaard once observed: "Despair is the sickness unto death ... the torment of despair is precisely this, not to be able to die."

What should a victim of major depression do? Fight? With what kind of weapon and what source of strength? Scream an angry stream of judgment against the disease and doctors and caretakers and God Himself? Or simply give up and give in?

When my depression put up its most vicious fight, my heart still told me not to give up. Yet my head told me that it was futile to try to fight it off in hopes of killing it with a thrust of whatever sword I could find. The lion was too mighty, too confident, too powerful, too persistent to die at my hands.

Thankfully, experience had taught me that I didn't have to sit by idly and let it devour me. The Holy Spirit blessed me with gifts that I could put to use in small, sometimes subtle, gradually progressive ways.

I didn't recognize them as gifts of the Spirit at the time I employed them. It was more a matter of the human instinct of survival. I had promised Donna, my children, and my friends that I wouldn't yield to those intermittent notions of suicide. That left me with the lone option of living with the depression, and that meant possibly abject melancholy more days than not and never a sampling of happiness.

I couldn't earn a living that way. I couldn't be a husband or father or friend that way. And I knew I couldn't be an authentic Christian that way.

I considered Jehoshaphat's story again. Yes, he failed to see any major offensive he could launch that effectively would conquer the foe. But his faith showed him some self-effacing attitudes and tactics.

He walked in the ways of his father, which had meant venerating God and removing all places of the worship of false gods. He observed whatever God had commanded. He respected God. He declared a fast of all his people.

That's what I needed to do. Forget looking for that elusive remedy that would put depression in my past. Instead, I took some advice from my wife and some friends in certain areas. And I listened to my heart on others.

The result: To go with the team I loosely had assembled, I also loosely assembled a game plan of relatively minor steps to take that at least would allow me to feel like I was doing something to help myself and not relying completely on the service of others.

In retrospect, the Holy Spirit really was at work the entire time by bestowing on me certain graces and gifts:

* * * * *

PATIENCE

"The Holy Spirit, who can be faster than any of us, is not in it for the quick hit. The Spirit counsels patience: you have all of eternity, and all that is not joy today will pass away someday. Remember that God wins in the end, and trust in that."

– Robert Longman Jr.

"Be patient, therefore, brothers, until the coming of the Lord. See how the farmer waits for the precious fruit of the earth, being patient with it until it receives the early and late rains. You too must be patient."

– James 5:7-8a

As of now, there is no cure for depression. At best, doctors and therapists can eliminate symptoms or hope the disease enters remission for a while. But no end of the symptoms or ability to manage the disease will happen immediately. Time will pass before life can return to some semblance of normalcy. It can be a slow, grueling, frustrating process.

It *is* a process. That's the key message to understand. It's about taking baby steps – not an easily acceptable fact for those of us used to running and rushing from one project to another, from one obligation to the next. You have to tolerate the new standards in life. What once seemed so simple, so routine, so taken for granted, now has to be viewed sometimes as a major victory.

When you are in the throes of major depression, celebrate getting out of bed some days. Rejoice over getting a shower. Recognize that, some days, just getting into the office is a major victory. When you look back at the end of the day, if you feel like the achievement in which you take most pride is that you made it to the end of the day, then write it down with gratitude.

I have been a list-maker my entire working life. I would end each day by writing down the list of all the tasks I hoped to accomplish the next day, in the next week and during the next month. I would update it each night. It usually was a long list of challenges, but I was pretty good at knocking things off routinely.

If that sounds at all like the kind of person you were before depression, don't make a list of tasks you need to accomplish any more. That only will lead to you staring at a list of failures. Be patient with yourself. Don't expect immediately to return to the man or woman you were before the disease struck. Cut yourself some slack.

My friend Jean made what turned out to be an amazingly helpful suggestion: The only list you should make is at the end of the day, when you jot down all the good things – great and small – that occurred that day. Donna tried the same technique with me when I felt my worst; she forced me to tell her one good thing that had happened. Do the same for yourself. Perhaps you ate two meals. You talked to a friend. You didn't cry as much as the day before. You worked a few hours. You laughed a little. You went to work and completed a couple of assignments. You listened to a bird sing for a while and found you enjoyed it.

Know that there probably will be moments that, after having taken a few small steps forward, you will get knocked back again, maybe even further than where you started. Tolerate it. There's nothing wrong with you other than you haven't licked the depression. It's still there, and it might not be departing any time soon.

One Biblical phrase often used interchangeably with patience is "long-suffering." Accept that reality; you might suffer for some time. During this period, focus even on the minor forward motion, not the blows that stopped you in your tracks or knocked you off your feet.

After a while, look back and compare what you were able to do six months or a year ago. You will see you actually have progressed.

*   *   *   *   *

HUMILITY

"Humility in a higher and ethical sense is that by which a man has a modest estimate of his own worth, and submits himself to others. ... A quality by which a person considering his own defects has a lowly opinion of himself and willingly submits himself to God and to others for God's sake."

– The New Advent Catholic Encyclopedia

"Take my yoke upon you and learn from me, for I am meek and humble of heart; and you will find rest for yourselves."

– Matthew 11:29

My parents did a terrific job preparing me for life. I was raised to believe that I was a gifted person, a strong person, one able to fend for himself in all situations. And I usually did. I finished college in three years. I was living on my own and working a fulltime job with great responsibility just a few months after graduation from the University of Missouri. I paid all my own bills and did well at everything. Self-sufficiency and maturity were proudly part of my character.

So it made sense that even in the midst of my depression at its worst, I kept thinking I should be able to beat it on my own.

At some point -- I'm not sure when -- I realized that one of the gifts God had given to me was a great many friends who truly wanted to help me. When Donna and I would share with some people what was going on in our lives, those friends and family members inevitably would offer to help in any way we needed. Usually, we thanked them and asked for their prayers. We didn't say more in part because we didn't really know how they could help. I also didn't want to seem weak and allow them to help, much less request their aid.

That ended one day when a revelation somehow helped me

understand that I wasn't being a good friend to those people if I didn't actually reach out to them, allow myself to be open to the grace of humility and acknowledge that I needed them.

I understood that my gifts couldn't push my wagon, that I needed to submit to the desire of friends and family to help pull it.

First, I let some of them into my world; I talked with them and revealed a hint about my life at the time. They didn't always understand the disease and its effects, but they listened with tender and caring hearts. Sharing my pain allowed us to become even more intimate as friends than we had been before.

Second, I made a list of those people – not including Donna, who already was helping more than I could have expected -- who genuinely had offered to help at some point and wrote down exactly what each of them did for me that made my life a little more tolerable. Jean was my sincere sounding board of unconditional love, someone who could listen and then tell me candidly, without fear of jeopardizing our friendship, what she thought. My sister Patti was a stay-at-home mom who could answer her phone almost any time during the day, so she could call to make sure I drank my orange juice each morning. My sister Marcia's son, Adam, is one of my godsons; she could help take my mind off myself for a while just by telling me what he was up to in life.

My friend Holly would share all the ups and downs of her day and ask my advice, allow me to be a friend to someone else. Larry and

Brian, who have become like the brothers I never had, engaged me in conversation about our faith journeys, let me share deeply about my love for God and actually prayed almost daily together for me. My mother-in-law had suffered from depression not much earlier, and two of my friends still were battling it; I could talk with them about bad days and find people who understood what I meant. My parents just wanted to hear my voice, letting me know I was important to someone.

After everything was compiled, I found myself with a diverse list of people and gifts they brought to my world. I told them what special thing they brought to my life that helped, and asked if they would fill that role for me. Each said yes. In some cases, they never needed to do what I had asked. But the important part was that I stepped out of myself for a bit and realized God had given me those people as genuine blessings. And the Lord was trying to teach me to rely on him and what he had sent into my life.

So do that, please. Make a list of the people in your life who truly care. Include some members of your family, include your closest friends, include some people you might not be particularly close to, but list all people who bring something special into your life *when you allow them.*

Then suck up your pride – which is the vice opposed to humility – and ask them to help in that special way.

You would do it for them, wouldn't you?

* * * * *

OBEDIENCE

"Obedience is the moral habit by which one carries out the order of his superior with the precise intent of fulfilling the injunction."

– New Advent Catholic Encyclopedia

"But Samuel said: 'Does the Lord so delight in holocausts and sacrifices as in obedience to the command of the Lord? Obedience is better than sacrifice.'"

-- 1 Samuel 15:22

All right, so you have prayed and considered thoughtfully the people you have selected to be your psychiatrist, your therapist, your spiritual director. You have your team – which, by the way, could also include a nutritionist, your primary care doctor, an exercise partner and anyone else who supports you. Just creating that ensemble actually is a major accomplishment.

So when your psychiatrist tells you to take a certain medication, why do you stop taking it? Is it because you feel a little better and think you don't need it any longer? Is it because you don't feel it's helping at all? Is it because something basically doesn't feel right about it, with side effects real or imagined?

Why, when your therapist convinces you to promise that you will take a walk each evening, do you do so only once in a while? Your therapist might have told you to write in your journal every night, or to make sure you call a friend when you are having a bad day, or to jot down every negative thought at the moment it enters your mind and then turn it into a written positive thought. What is keeping you from following those directions most days?

Your spiritual director may have recommended that you feel free to ask God why He is allowing these bad things to happen to you. Why do you avoid that conversation in prayer? Is it because you feel guilty talking to God that way?

Each of those people on your team is either a professional or special friend in whom you placed a certain level of trust. They have knowledge and connections and gifts that generally will far outweigh anything you could gather in a relatively short period of time. If you say you trust them, then trust them!

I don't always practice what I preach in this area. I have stopped taking my medication at times, and at other times I took more than I was supposed to take for reasons that only could hurt myself. Once, so desperate to get some kind of prolonged sleep, I took my sleep medication every two hours for 14 hours. The result was that I didn't sleep any better but I had a severe reaction: an incredible increase in the depressive feelings. And there was that time when I surreptitiously stockpiled various pills for several days, added them to some heavy painkillers I had found, then after downing all of them drank a few large glasses of wine. That forced me back into an undesired stay on the sixth floor of the hospital and a night I don't really remember at all.

All because I disobeyed.

My therapist knew it was ridiculous to tell me to begin exercising an hour a day at the local YMCA when I never had been a workout kind of a guy. Still, she knew some kind of physical activity was vital to improving my disposition. So she got me to vow I would take a walk, two to six blocks through my neighborhood, each night. But I didn't always take my evening walk or write in my journal each night or face the negative thoughts that were filling my mind.

I talked with my spiritual director, Father Jeff, about my desire to set aside prayer time each day. That made me feel better on days I stuck to it. But I refused to allow myself to get angry with God openly when, in my heart, there was some disappointment in His decision not to cure me. So I strayed from even simple prayer sometimes.

In each case, the results of not doing just the minimal acts were not good. I would plunge even deeper into despair, cry more easily, find myself assuming my life never would improve.

In each case, once I realized that in not following the instructions of the experts I was actually disobeying the Almighty God who had sent them into my life to help, I tried to abide by their directions.

* * * * *

SIMPLICITY

"As a character trait, (simplicity is) the quality of not being affected; therefore, unassuming and unpretentious. A simple person is honest, sincere and straightforward. Simplicity is single-mindedness. As a supernatural virtue it seeks only to do the will of God without regard to self-sacrifice or self-advantage."

– The Pocket Catholic Dictionary

"The Lord protects the simple; I was helpless, but God saved me."

– Psalm 116:6

Perhaps the most notable aspect of the life of St. Teresa of Avila was, as one author called it, "the treasure of the Holy Spirit that allowed her to just pay attention to God." That could be simplicity in its most evident form as it relates to a faith-filled life.

So how can a victim of depression help himself by pursuing such an uncomplicated approach? I have discerned four easy, natural ways:

- Worship. If possible, attend Mass or the worship service at the church of your choice on a regular basis. Worshipping God helps us understand how we relate to him, and doing it as a group enables us to recognize that as such, we form the Body of Christ. That gives us the possibility of tapping into his ability to create, heal and renew. It allows us to reach beyond ourselves, to declare before and with others that we believe God to be all-powerful and all-worthy of our praise. Experiencing worship as a community, and feeling that experience, knowing you are part of a family of believers, will lift your spirits more than you realize.

- **Sing.** A friend of mine was feeling particularly beaten up by life one morning. He heard God telling him to sing. "I don't want to sing," Don told God. "Sing anyway," God replied. He did, and in time he felt better because of it. Singing is one of the simplest yet most profound activities you can pursue. The Bible tells us to sing more often than it tells us to pray. God wants to hear us praise him, thank him, ask him, implore him, cry to him, acknowledge him in song. Sing whatever you like or know – an old hymn, a contemporary Christian song, a prayer from Mass, your favorite classic rock love ballad. God doesn't care what it is. Just that it is. It's a sweet sound to his ear, whether you whisper it or sing it at the top of your lungs. Yes, sing often, and do it even if you don't think you have much of a voice. The quality of the performance doesn't matter. Remember, he gave you the voice. He knows what you sound like. To him, it's the most delightful sound he ever created.

- Listen to Music. Forget singing for a while. Turn on some favorite music – perhaps uplifting and joyful, perhaps meditative and prayerful, perhaps something that has no obvious spiritual dimension at all – and just enjoy letting it soak into your soul. Maybe it will be classical music that takes your mind to places you don't even comprehend. Or it could be contemporary Christian music that speaks to some spiritual dimension of your life, that helps you find some insight or direction. You also might consider playing songs that, in a better and happier time of your life, meant something to you – maybe that background music that filled your days of high school and college years. Or the day you first knew you were loved by God.

- Pray. There will be many, many times when you just won't want to do it. Conversation with God will be the last thing you will desire. You might find yourself angry with him. You might find yourself questioning, if not his existence, then at least his choices. You might find yourself clothed in guilt that you haven't spent time in prayer and thus don't know how or where to begin. Or you might find the idea of reading the Bible or reciting longer prayers or having an extended talk with the Lord to be more than your current strength can bear. But prayer is more than a good idea; it's absolutely necessary for you to make any progress toward emerging from that hopelessness you feel.

It's for that reason that I created what I call my "Prayer Gems." I bought a notebook small enough to fit into the pocket of my shirt, the back pocket of my pants or tuck into my Bible cover. I tote it with me wherever I go.

During the course of a few months of really struggling with my depression, I found I needed some words of encouragement or short prayers to say or ideas to express to God that spoke from a distressed heart. As I flipped through the Bible or read some books I had, I found snippets that I wrote on each page of the little notebook. The result is 150 pages of a variety of extremely short readings, prayers and selections from the Bible, Christian writers, the Liturgy of the Hours and various saints.

After saying my Morning Prayer and taking my shower, I randomly open my Prayer Gems. Sometimes, the words on that first page truly resonate with whatever my mood is that day. Other times, it just doesn't seem to reflect the words on my heart at the moment, so I turn the pages until I find the one that says exactly what I feel.

Some provide hope amid my depression: *For you know that the testing of your faith produces perseverance. ... It is not the will of your heavenly Father that one of these little ones be lost. ... My God has sent his* angel and closed the lions' mouths so that they have not hurt me. ... God not only loves me as I am, but knows me as I am.

Some echo my deep depression of the day and simply cry out to God: *Free us from the desires that belong to the darkness. ... Stand by me, God; do not forsake me; do not abandon me, my Savior. ... Save me from the lion's mouth.*

Some are merely short-but-sweet prayers that give me a chance to talk with God when I don't have the concentration or inner power to imagine more than a few words: *God, come to my assistance; Lord, make haste to help me. ... Do not stay far from me, for trouble is near, and there is no one to help. ... Be gone, Satan!*

Inevitably, the prayer I say or thoughts I read at the beginning of the day become my background music and thoughts the rest of the day. I open the notebook to that page often over the rest of the morning, afternoon and evening. Sometimes, I read the words so often that I've memorized them as a prayer I recite in particularly difficult moments. Or one word will leap out, and I find my mind whispering it often in my subconscious throughout the day.

Some become so important that they become ingrained in me every day thereafter. For instance, on one particular morning I was on the verge of becoming completely exhausted by the ups and downs of the disease, fed up with having to battle it unexpectedly sometimes, wanting to make things happen immediately. And then I opened the notebook to a page with this prayer from St. Francis of Assisi:

"Jesus suffered patiently because he suffered for me. O Jesus, gracious Lamb of God, I renounce forever my impatience. I commit my destiny to you, resigning myself to your holy will."

I found myself whispering those words the rest of the day, at one point knowing in my heart that St. Francis was praying it with me. And my impatience seemed to evaporate.

More than anything, the "Prayer Gems" have given me a way to maintain and even deepen my relationship with God during a time when I don't feel much like working on *any* relationships. It has enabled me to sense his Presence constantly throughout each day, to feel his power when I have none at all. To be reminded that he's helping me through an extremely challenging part of my life.

*   *   *   *   *

WISDOM

"Wisdom means knowledge that is so perfect it directs the will to obey God's commands."

– The Pocket Catholic Dictionary.

"Happy is the man who finds wisdom, the man who gains understanding"

– Proverbs 3:13

You have a disease – or your loved one is burdened with a disease

– that isn't completely understood by even the most learned members of the medical community. Doctors and researchers aren't universally convinced what causes clinical depression, even less convinced of what treatments can lessen it or wipe it out.

That doesn't mean you have to rely entirely on the information that comes from your doctors. Yes, their advice is vital. But you don't have to blindly settle for what they say as the final word of knowledge about depression. New research is happening all the time. New drugs and new treatment are in development. New methods of talk therapy are being pursued.

Donna has become something of an expert on the subject of major depression. She's not a doctor and doesn't profess to be ready to ignore medical advice. But she has found – thanks to the internet – plenty of alternative ideas to try along with the drugs and therapy I'm employing. Nothing crazy, mind you. For instance, I have been a major drinker of Diet Coke for many years. Donna read that aspartame, the sweetener used in Diet Coke, has been linked to possibly helping exacerbate depression; so I agreed to stop drinking it.

I tried visiting a chiropractor and undergoing acupuncture in part because of reports that they could help reduce depression. I used certain vitamin supplements because they helped a friend's mother-in-law not only emerge from depression but sleep much better.

Now, please be careful. Always check with your doctor or pharmacist before pursuing alternative treatments, but don't be afraid to investigate them using reputable sources to form the right questions.

And you shouldn't limit your research and information to treatments. Donna knows the possible side effects and things that can cause reactions to my medications as well as doctors and pharmacists, so she knows what I need to avoid eating or doing. She also is more intimately knowledgeable about my eating habits and other routines, meaning she can anticipate situations better than medical professionals who see me for 15 minutes or an hour a month.

A good psychiatrist and talk therapist are essential; no outside treatment should be attempted without consulting them first, too. But you, or someone with greater strength, owe it to yourself to explore some other possibilities and then challenge the medical people to consider them.

* * * * *

COMPASSION

"We define compassion as a feeling of sorrow or concern for another person's suffering or need accompanied by a subsequent desire to alleviate the suffering."

– Researchers at the University of California-Berkeley

"When he disembarked and saw the vast crowd, he was moved with compassion for them, for they were like sheep without a shepherd."

– Mark 6:34

One of the biggest challenges facing a victim of depression is that constant sense of self-absorption. You don't even realize it, but your ears and your mind and your heart slowly become shut off to the lives of others. It happens in such a subtle way. A friend will mention their personal struggle of the time or a concern in their life, and the depth of their heartache might not register with you. A family member might encounter a stumbling block or a brick wall in life, and you simply don't notice.

In part, that could be the result of friends and family not wanting to share their problems with you because they aren't sure if you can handle them, given your sickness and emotional instability. Nice of them to care so much. Shame on them for not giving you a chance to love them.

You need to push away from concerns about yourself and notice there are other people in the world, people in your own life who can use the gifts you have to offer them. Make a point of every morning telling yourself you are going to pay attention to the people you meet that day – family, friends, co-workers, people at the gas station or the fast-food restaurant. Ask about their lives. Sincerely ask and wait for an answer.

I made a true effort of doing that at a certain point. If a client told me they would be having surgery the following week, I told them I would pray for them. And I did. If someone did something nice for me, I sent them a thank-you note. If a friend had a story to tell, I listened – really listened.

The results helped begin a turnaround in my life.

For instance, I always stopped at a certain convenience store on my way into the office each morning. During those two months during and immediately after I underwent the ECT treatments, obviously I wasn't stopping there at all for my daily Diet Coke with Lime. When I returned to my routine, the woman who worked there in the mornings asked where I had been for so long; I made up some story about my hours changing and habits changing for a while. I felt guilty, though. So I wrote her a card, thanking her for always giving me a smile and some friendly words to begin my day and explaining in vague terms that I actually had been sick during those two months. On the visit subsequent to my giving her the card, she pulled me aside and asked, if it wasn't an intrusion, about my sickness. I decided to be honest and told her I had depression.

"You know," she said, "I think I might have that, too."

That initiated a conversation that turned into a little friendship. I helped her understand the importance of visiting a doctor at least to talk about her symptoms. She ended up taking anti-depressants for a while and feeling much better.

I re-connected with an old friend from high school. I shared my problem with him, and he shared his relentless battle with bi-polar disease. That turned into an important relationship. We found that if we called each other and asked how things were going, if one of us said, "I'm having a pretty bad day," the other immediately understood what that meant in ways that most other people in our life simply couldn't. We wouldn't engage in a two-man pity party with each other; rather, we could listen with a legitimately empathetic heart.

I went to a graduation party one afternoon and saw an old friend with whom I hadn't talked for a while, someone who didn't know about my depression. She hadn't been returning phone calls. Before I even could ask why, she pulled me aside and explained that she had been experiencing a severe bout with depression the last few months. As soon as I told her I understood and why, that connection immediately helped her feel she had found someone who could listen not just to her words and her feelings, but to the reality of her life.

That day, I didn't say a word about my struggles. I simply listened.

Pay attention to the suffering in the lives of those God sends to cross your path. Open yourself to them. Let their pain move you. Know that you can help.

* * * * *

MERCY

"The disposition to be kind and forgiving. Founded on compassion, mercy differs from compassion or the feeling of sympathy in putting this feeling into practice with a readiness to assist. It is therefore the ready willingness to help anyone in need, especially in need of pardon or reconciliation."

– *The Pocket Catholic Dictionary*

"Blessed are the merciful, for they shall obtain mercy."

– *Matthew 5:7*

When I examined myself and my life -- something every depression victim does often because he finds himself alone with his thoughts so often -- I didn't like what I saw. I deemed myself a huge imposition in the life of my wife, who deserved a husband to care for her and love her rather than a husband who evoked sympathy and concern. My children deserved the dad they *used* to have, one who joked and provided guidance and was a pillar of stability.

So many things in that vein. It was difficult not to feel like a failure, a sinner of disproportionate measure, a man who wasn't really a man at all.

The Hebrew word translated as "mercy" is used 149 times in the Old Testament and 59 times in the New Testament. Tom Stewart, writing in 1999 on his website www.whatsaiththescripture.com, said, "Mercy is not simply the withholding of punishment, but it is the act of giving help or having compassion on someone who is afflicted." Clearly, it's an important aspect of the character of God, one we view as an amazing gift provided us.

We know we should display mercy toward others. We should help others who are hurting. We should help them find forgiveness and reconciliation when those actions feel foreign, when that vacancy is holding them back from fully experiencing God's love and the love of others. When we have been hurt by others, we should not only forgive them but reach out with kindness and help them feel that we still love them.

But how about showing *ourselves* a little mercy? How about forgiving *ourselves* for the difficulties we present in the lives of others? Yes, our depression affects those around us. That's not your choice, though. You didn't decide to suffer from the disease and thus make life challenging for your family, friends, co-workers – and yourself.

If there is some sin you know you have committed, against God and man, then confess, seek the reconciliation that is waiting for you, allow Jesus Christ to lift that burden off your shoulders and hurl it into the sea of forgetfulness.

And once that's done, it's done. The disease likely won't disappear that quickly, but you can quit taking any more blame for your depression. Absolve yourself. Be kind to yourself rather than criticizing yourself, rather than assuming the disease defines you. Help yourself. Identify the things that will help, even in the smallest way, and hunt them down. And don't feel guilty about pursuing a healthy life. You might never find perfect happiness; none of us are promised that. Some of the things that triggered your depression might not be reversed easily (such as loss of a job) or changed at all (such as the death of a loved one).

But forgive yourself for the way you reacted to those things in life. Know that you are not alone in your suffering. Understand that what ultimately has happened involves some brain chemistry and life events that went wacky.

Depression is not your fault. The fallout from it is not your fault.

Have mercy on yourself.

God has. He has given you the gifts to help live with your depression, to slowly and patiently make progress climbing out of the pit of despair. He has shown not only kindness and compassion, but he has provided the readiness to carry you.

He is a merciful God. No matter what you believe you cannot do, he believes differently. Like Jehoshaphat, all you need do is to acknowledge your helplessness.

Pray with me, please:

So often in life, my God, we think we should have the answers to our problems rather than rely on you for those answers. We don't think about asking for help, either from you or those you have sent into our life. Father, I come to you now acknowledging that I am at a loss what to do. I need your assistance. Have mercy on me, wash me white as snow. Grant me the humility to embrace being your child and to accept your gift of love.

***   ***   ***   ***   ***

TAKING ACTION: Turn to this section near the back of the book. Find the action points that correspond with this chapter and try to commit yourself to following the suggestions.

CHAPTER NINE:

REST STOP – THE GOOD GOD

A story is told about St. John Vianney, whose first and only assignment as a priest was as the pastor of the church in the small French village of Ars – thus his well-known title of Cure d'Ars. Every day, the Cure d'Ars would see an old gentleman just sitting for hours in the church. Finally, one day the priest asked the man what he was doing there for so long.

"I look at the good God," the old man replied, "and the good God looks at me."

The good God looks at us everywhere we go. That includes those times when we step into misery, when we wander lost into the wilderness, when we meander fearfully through the desert stretches of life. When we are afraid, when we don't trust as we should, when we don't notice his Presence as obviously as we would desire.

Consider two entries from my prayer journal.

For the first, I had read the Gospel selection from that morning's

Mass, Matthew 17:14-20.

When they came to the crowd a man approached, knelt down before (Jesus), and said, "Lord, have pity on my son, for he is a lunatic (note: possibly an epileptic) and suffers severely; often he falls into fire, and often into water. I brought him to your disciples, but they did not cure him." Jesus said in reply, "O faithless and perverse generation, how long will I be with you? How long will I endure you? Bring him here to me." Jesus rebuked him and the demon came out of him, and from that hour the boy was cured.

After reading that, pondering that and praying about that, I wrote the following:

"I pray every day for my children. Well, I try to make it every day formally, but the requests for them are in my heart every day, every moment. I ask for God to care for them, for his will to be done in their lives and for me to be the parent he wants me to be.

"But I find that I fall into worry. I fret. I've been doing it a lot more lately. Again. I regret that I haven't been a better dad to Jessica and Josh, that there is a disconnect there that causes me, selfishly, to miss them and to worry that I haven't given them what they need. I regret, selfishly, that Erin will be going away to school and I will miss her greatly. I am concerned that I've asked and allowed Kara to take on too much in life, that she has grown away from me.

"Then today, I read of a father who went to Jesus and 'knelt before him,' asked Jesus to heal his son who was ill and sometimes even fell into fire and fell into water. I still worry that my children will experience the equivalent of being burned or drown in this life, as they make poor decisions or get overwhelmed, that they will fall away from their faith and that I haven't been a good enough father to keep all that from happening. The dad in this Gospel story didn't try to solve the problem himself, at least not any more. He had even stopped asking the apostles for help – going to your church community won't solve all problems. Lost in what could well have been described as a desert of despair, his last hope, he took his plea straight to Christ and humbled himself and faithfully asked for the healing.

"I prayed about that. And God spoke to me. I clearly heard his Voice. He said, 'You pray to me all the time to take care of your children, then you take the responsibility back. Let me take care of them. Have faith that I will. As much as you love them, and I know you love them a great deal, I love them even more. I want what is best for them. I know what is best for them, and I am with them all the time. Kneel before me in all your faith, which only needs to be the size of a mustard seed, and then taste the patience my Spirit has given you. Your children will be fine. They love you. In time, my time, you will see this clearly. But know this now because I have told you."

In an arid region of my soul, God taught me.

He taught me again about a month later, when I was lost in a dark pit of remorse. On that day, I wrote:

"God's grace amazes me.

"It comes when you aren't really expecting it, in ways strange and mysterious – and sometimes kind of funny. Yes, his sense of humor shows up in the most graceful ways. For instance … this evening, I went to our parish to receive the Sacrament of Reconciliation. (For non-Catholics, you might have heard it called "Confession." True enough, we do confess sins to a priest. But the beauty of the sacrament lies in Jesus Christ, through the ministry of the priest, providing absolution of those sins we commit on a regular basis, those times when we have hurt the Body of Christ in his Church, and we are thus reconciled with that Church.)

"I had felt a growing sense of my sinfulness over the course of the three previous days. As I have gradually felt more and more the Presence of God in all things and all people, and felt his Love in an even deeper and richer way, I also found myself sensing greater guilt about offending God in heaven, in all things and all people, with my lies, my lust, my selfishness, my pride, my inability to surrender completely to him. I had noticed that I couldn't even look people in the eyes after a while without some effort; in their eyes I would see the God I had betrayed.

"So in tears, I confessed my guilt and the sources of my guilt. I released in words the burden I had been carrying. And I was forgiven.

Like that. Jesus Christ forgave me and tossed every one of those sins away forever. Gone.

"My only assigned task from the priest – my penance, if you will – was to accept that. To try to sin no more, sure. But to accept that God – in heaven, in all things and all people, within myself – loves me in my sinfulness. I vowed to try.

"I knelt in church for a few moments, thanking God for the cherished gift of being able to confess my failings and find forgiveness once more. And then I walked back into the world outside in search of genuine reconciliation in real life.

"Being close to dinner time, I drove to the nearby Jack-In-The-Box. (Yes, Donna, I ordered a salad.) When the young man handed the sack of my food to me, he also handed me one of those little ornaments to put on the top of your car antenna. This one was adorned for a New Year's celebration. Silly. Foolish. Goofy. I never would have asked for one, probably never would have thought even to want one.

"The young man said, 'Here's a Jack ball. Guaranteed to put a smile on your face and make you happy.' Smiling already, I looked the innocent young man in the eyes. 'Thank you,' I said.

"What a concept: the Grace of God finding me in the wilderness at a fast-food restaurant drive-through."

Indeed, wherever you happen to be, you can look at the good God and the good God will be looking at you.

Pray with me, please:

I am always on your mind, always in your sight, Lord. Thank you. You are with me in forgiveness, in laughter, in the embrace from my children, in the kiss from my wife. Thank you. You speak through smiles and tears, nature and your Word. Thank you, Lord. Simply help me to pay attention.

***   ***   ***   ***   ***

TAKING ACTION: Turn to this section near the back of the book. Find the action points that correspond with this chapter and try to commit yourself to following the suggestions.

CHAPTER TEN:

"HENCE MY EYES ARE TURNED TOWARD YOU"

"We're given gifts," professional baseball player Mike Matheny once told me. "What we do with those gifts is an opportunity to give back to God, to worship Him.

"We're left with a high responsibility."

And the feeling that comes when we fall short, when we think we have failed … when we wander into a desert and don't know which direction to turn …

Those in management with the St. Louis Cardinals baseball team took some grief from fans when they signed Matheny as a free agent in December 1999. His major-league career hadn't exactly inspired predictions of playing regularly for any good team or gaining a spot in an All-Star Game. Frankly, some thought he was lucky to be playing in the big leagues at all. One of his previous managers once watched Matheny taking batting practice and actually said, "I can't watch. Tell me when it's over."

Matheny had a paltry .229 career batting average and all of 22 home runs after his first six years in the majors. For those unfamiliar with baseball statistics, that's something inferior to "not very good."

But in the eyes of the wisest baseball scouts, Matheny brought value that went well beyond an ability to hit a baseball. He was an outstanding defensive catcher. Technically, he did everything to near perfection. What's more, he had an intellect for the game, a work ethic and an attitude for relentless preparation that enabled him to help pitchers perform better than even they expected of themselves.

He was a leader, on the field and in the clubhouse. He exuded a humble confidence, held strong beliefs and didn't hesitate to stand up for those beliefs. Matheny nurtured younger players and protected his teammates with unrelenting support.

That's what the Cardinals wanted when they brought him to the team for the 2000 season. They essentially told him, "You are going to be our starting catcher. You are going to be our team leader. You are important to us."

I remember talking with Matheny in the Cardinals' clubhouse

in Jupiter, Florida, with only three weeks remaining in spring training 2000. He should have been on top of the world. That contract he had signed with the Cardinals had given him a chance to call home and say, "Dad, you can quit your job. You'll never have to work again." He had married a gal from the St. Louis area, and for the first time he would be able to live year-round and play in the same city. Kristin, his wife, had just left Florida to return home to St. Louis, where the Mathenys had four children – and Kristin was expecting No. 5.

But Mike felt something close to desperation.

He couldn't hit. His batting average for spring-training games was even worse than usual. He couldn't catch. His defensive prowess hadn't lived up to promise. And he didn't feel like he could be a team leader when he was worried about making the team.

Matheny went back to his hotel room. He couldn't remember a time when he had felt so alone and afraid.

"I was just stinking," Matheny said in retrospect a few months later. "It wasn't about squandering anything. I just stunk."

The Cardinals had other catchers. There was a young hot-shot who had great hitting potential. There was an older catcher who had plenty of experience.

Matheny knew a cold darkness. He had been trying to do

everything on his own, relying on his ability to make the most of his God-given talents. His way wasn't working.

So he turned his eyes toward God.

"There was a moment of revelation for me," he said. "I was at the team hotel, and I had a lot of time with my thoughts, my prayers, my Bible. All of a sudden, I realized an opportunity was slipping away.

"I realized it was time to put it all on the line and sink or swim."

Matheny decided he couldn't achieve anything on his own strength. So he placed complete trust in the Almighty God. Already a strong Christian, Matheny surrendered all his desire and ability to Jesus Christ.

He adopted a song by Steven Curtis Chapman as a theme for his baseball season. Eventually, a piece of that song, "Dive," was played at the Cardinals' Busch Stadium each time Matheny went to bat. In part, the song says:

> *"So if you'll take my hand/We'll close our eyes and count to three*
>
> *And take the leap of faith/Come on, let's go"*

In the darkness, Mike Matheny rediscovered a dependence upon God. He cast all his cares upon him, took God's hand and trusted to be led to whatever place God thought Matheny needed to go.

The Cardinals' catcher went on to play 120 games during the 2000 regular season. He batted .261 and drove in 47 runs, best in his career. Every pitcher with the team credited Matheny for making them better than they ever envisioned. He won the award for best defensive catcher in the National League.

Jehoshaphat could have saved Mike some worry. Not that Matheny learned anything he didn't already know. But even the best of Christians forget when life's reality knocks them back on their heels. They find that putting faith into practice can become a daunting contest.

People face hard times. They wake up and their world doesn't feel familiar any longer. They are afraid, uncertain, tentative, filled with doubt. They look for a way back to the comfortable but find they are blind. They reach for security and find they are grasping at emptiness. They seek a life filled with satisfaction and nourishment but discover the new neighborhood scorched and barren.

Every victim of major depression knows such distress. Like Jehoshaphat, not one of them asked to be there.

Please know that not all Christians have taken the attitude that major depression is a choice rather than a disease. For one, the esteemed Oswald Chambers wrote in "My Utmost For His Highest" that "if we were never depressed, we would not be alive – only material things don't suffer depression. If human beings were not capable of depression, we would have no capacity for happiness and exaltation."

Human beings weren't made with a guarantee to be happy or to have success in the eyes of man. We weren't created merely for the drudgery of work, eat, sleep, do it all again. We weren't made just for play or laughter, either. And we certainly weren't given breath in order to suffer all our days.

No, we were made to have life. That encompasses all those things. Laughter and tears. Joy and grief. Work and play. Sowing and reaping. Activity and rest. We will have days of happiness and comfort. We will know the ecstasy of welcoming new life. We also will know death, fear, disappointment, frustration.

And thank God that we do.

"Isn't life full of a lot of loneliness and misery and all those things?" the late songwriter Rich Mullins once said. "But who wants to give it up? Nobody. It's a wonderful thing. Isn't it great to have legs?"

Give a creature legs, a brain and a soul, and the possibilities are endless. We can walk up the aisle on our wedding day, the center of attention and filled with all sorts of plans and hopes and dreams. We can run after a laughing child, scoop him up in our arms and share in the joy of the moment. We can walk into an office and take responsibility. We can jump after a basketball or volleyball, or leap to grab an apple off a tree.

Legs. What a simple gift we have been given. Same for our arms, our hearts, our minds … our souls.

Each a blessing.

But what makes us human makes us exposed to difficulties. And for that we can praise God with all the strength we can muster.

In his enlightening and inspiring book about Abraham Lincoln's decades-long depression – which apparently lasted even until his assassination – Joshua Wolf Shenk observed that Lincoln's remarkable leadership and decisions might have represented his response to his illness, "the visible end of Lincoln's effort to contain his dark feelings and thoughts, to wrestle privately with his moods until they passed or lightened."

Shenk said that psychologist David B. Cohen has written, "With depression, recovery may be a matter of shifting from protest to more effective ways of mastering helplessness." Thus, concludes Shenk, Lincoln's greatness might not have been a matter of attaining victory over his suffering or because he found a means to cure his depression. Rather, he integrated the lessons he gained from his struggle with melancholy and used those lessons "as all the more fuel for the fire of his great work."

Thomas Merton, writing in his book "Thoughts in Solitude," called it a wasteland.

"The desert," he said, "was the region in which the Chosen People had wandered for forty years, cared for by God alone. They could have reached the Promised Land in a few months if they had traveled directly to it. God's plan was that they should learn to love him in the wilderness and that they should always look back on the time in the desert as the idyllic time of their life with him alone."

The celebrated poet Robert Frost certainly was familiar with the darkness of life. One of his children committed suicide. Another was so severely struck by mental illness that she was institutionalized. Knowing that allows you to read the following excerpt from his poem "Acquainted With The Night," and enables you to feel his agony.

> *"I have been one acquainted with the Night*
> *I have walked out in rain – and back in rain.*
> *I have outwalked the furthest city light.*
> *I have looked down the saddest city lane."*

As Father Matthew Kelty observed in speaking once to his fellow members of the Trappist Monastery in Gethsemani, Kentucky, becoming acquainted with the night is not a plunge into desperate darkness because, he said, "Without the night, one does not see the stars."

Or, as American poet Theodore Roethke said, "In a dark time, the eye begins to see."

Yes, it feels like absolute darkness, blacker than black. And it feels so very lonely, more frightening than can be explained. It is from this darkness that a victim of depression loses touch with hope, when people might turn into such a miserable spouse that divorce occurs, might fail so miserably to meet job requirements that they are fired, might lose touch with abilities as parent and friend to the point of guilt and abject isolation.

It is from this darkness that victims of depression consider suicide.

Darkness need not be an enemy, though. Jehoshaphat teaches us that. When he first encountered the news of those local armies coming after his people, the king declared a fast. Not just for himself, but for his entire nation. One of the reasons the Hebrew people would engage in a fast was to achieve atonement for sins and hope to avert some impending catastrophe.

Many Christians will choose to fast in order to find a closer intimacy with God. Jesus fasted for 40 days and 40 nights in the desert before Satan's three temptations. Jesus often went into the desert or off by himself, away from the influences of the world. There, he sought a special closeness with his Father. He sought strength. He sought direction.

As did Jehoshaphat. While in the darkness, Jehoshaphat came to realize he had only one real choice: He had to look to God for help.

In "The Depression Book: Depression as an Opportunity for Spiritual Growth," writer Cheri Huber actually calls depression a gift, an ally, because it has something to teach the victim.

"Depression brings me back to myself in a way much of life does not," Huber wrote. "It gets my attention. It says, 'Stop! Pay attention!'"

Pay attention to what?

To the good God. To a Father, a Savior, a friend who simply wants to be Present to us. To a Teacher who wants to show us something, reveal something, give us something. To the Almighty Creator who simply wants to remind us to depend upon Him alone.

Charles Swindoll, in his book "Paul: A Man of Grace and Grit," devotes one chapter to studying St. Paul's trip on the Mediterranean Sea to Rome, a trip that met with a vicious storm and shipwreck at Malta. Swindoll wrote:

"The storms we endure may last for days, weeks, months or even years. Perfect storms are largely unpredictable. They rage on with seemingly no end in sight. Often, they appear wildly out of control. ... You may be there now. ...

"Where you find yourself is not the result of an accident, nor are you alone. God is neither absent nor indifferent. You are precisely where he planned for you to be at this very moment. He could have calmed your storm at any point, but he hasn't. Your situation may appear as close to impossible to you as it can get. Like the sailors and passengers of Paul's ill-fated ship, you may be wringing your hands, waiting for the light of day. I repeat, that isn't accidental.

"Allow me to move from the stinging spray blasting its way across the deck of that ship mentioned in Acts 27 to the real-world storm you may now be facing. Questions emerge as fear grows within. Panic thoughts make you uneasy. How do you keep it together?"

Swindoll noted that during the most frightful part of the storm faced by Paul and the others on that ship, the sailors tossed out four anchors to keep them from crashing into land -- and certain death -- they could not see. The author suggested that when we face personal storms, we also toss out four anchors: of stability in what God has said in Scripture; of unity, as you rely on the help of others; of renewal, which he notes comes primarily through prayer; and of reality, which means doing whatever hard work is necessary to get through. He noted that could mean finding humility in the face of God and other people, getting some professional counseling and seeking reconciliation with someone.

Saint John of the Cross knew the valuable experience of darkness when he wrote his classic book "Dark Night of the Soul." Yes, the title implies a frightening encounter with an absence of God, even a questioning of his existence. But the saint meant something quite the opposite.

"These times of aridity cause the soul to journey in all purity in the love of God, since it is no longer influenced in its actions by the pleasure and sweetness of the actions themselves," he wrote, "but only by a desire to please God. ... There grows within souls that experience this arid night (of the senses) care for God and yearnings to serve him, for in proportion as the breasts of sensuality, wherewith it sustained and nourished the desires that it pursued, are drying up, there remains nothing in that aridity and detachment save the yearning to serve God, which is a thing very pleasing to God."

When all is darkness, there is only one place to turn. That is all God wants of us in those moments. When we despair, when we feel incompetent, discouraged and doomed, he only wants us to recognize him.

Wrote T.S. Eliot: "I said to my soul be still, and let the darkness come upon you, which shall be the darkness of God."

So don't fear the storms of your life or the pit of grief and fear into which you will fall during episodes of depression. When you feel certain that there is no other choice, embrace that time -- because you still have one choice, the choice that ultimately will change everything.

"Darkness is depression, dark thoughts, a dark hole, a dark day," writes Raymond Lloyd Richmond, in his "Guide to Psychology and Its

Practice." He proceeds to note that one way to refute such metaphors is to replace them as he says, "Darkness can represent the womb as well as the tomb. Darkness is where life begins. Darkness is our time of building strength and gathering powers for future use. Darkness is comfort and security. Darkness is a time of rest and quiet.

"Darkness is a good thing not to be wished away or battled against but to be enjoyed."

The depression certainly doesn't feel enjoyable when you are beset by tears and anxiety and utter desolation. All that's left is to seek God.

Pray with me, please:

I lack the strength, the knowledge, the tools, the ability to emerge from this difficult time on my own, Lord. So I am prepared to take a leap of faith. I have nowhere else to turn. Hence, my eyes are turned toward you.

*** *** *** *** ***

TAKING ACTION: Turn to this section near the back of the book. Find the action points that correspond with this chapter and try to commit yourself to following the suggestions.

CHAPTER ELEVEN:

REST STOP – THE GRASS UNDER THE GREAT OAK TREE

Shade and dogs can prove menacing to the idea of growing grass.

Such has been my experience in our backyard. The lawn always has looked sparse beneath the great oak back there ever since we moved into the home in 2000. Sure, the tremendous shade helped keep the rear section of the house and patio somewhat cooler during the hot, sunny days of summer. But to let virtually no direct sunlight slip through during spring and summer because of that constant shadow and then in the fall because of its deep coat of dropped leaves, the great tree really didn't give any grass a prospect at life.

Then, there was Trixie. Our Australian shepherd's chain was tethered just off the edge of the patio. She liked to sit under the oak and watch the world pass down the street. When she would pace or run, she wore down what little grass had bravely endured until all that remained was an extensive patch of dirt -- mud when it rained -- stretching from the base of the tree down the incline a few dozen feet to well into the center of the concrete patio.

Dirt. Mud. Essentially a lifeless wasteland of earth.

Not that I'm much of a lush lawn guy. Usually my yard has the most hideous look in the neighborhood. Often I won't cut it until the grass tickles the ankles. I never spread seed or fertilizer, rarely bother even to try to kill the weeds and dandelions. I told myself and others it had to do with lack of time, that I was too busy with important things. It was only grass, after all.

Something in my thoughts changed a few years ago. I had finished kicking up some grimy powder mowing the weeds and dirt under the oak one spring day. A revelation struck. I had had enough of looking at that desert.

"I'll be back in a little bit," I told Donna. "I'm going to get some grass seed."

"But it's spring. You're supposed to do that in the fall," she protested.

Like I expected it would make a difference. "I don't care," I said. "I'm tired of that bare spot out there."

Of course, I had no clue what I was doing. I got to the home and garden store, and began wandering aimlessly through the aisles. You might as well have asked me to build an airplane or solve an electrical wiring problem. Completely clueless, probably dangerously so.

As fate would have it, I accidentally happened upon some large bags of grass seed stacked high off to one side. Was it the right kind of seed? The type of grass I would want? My eyes scanned the bag and these words, in large letters, immediately grabbed my attention: SURVIVES SHADED AREAS. Aha! I tossed the heavy sack over my left shoulder, picked up a hand-held spreader, anxiously paid for them and with a surprising enthusiasm headed for home.

I couldn't wait. As soon as I arrived back at the house, I ripped open the bag. Suddenly, a flood of questions and doubts came to mind: How much should I put on each bare area? Should I use more, considering it was April and not October? What was I doing, thinking April-sown grass could make it through a Missouri summer? Donna probably was right. What did the bag say? "SURVIVES HEAT." Really? OK, I'll believe the bag.

So off I went. I scooped up some seed in the spreader, started turning the crank and smiled as the little bits of future life went flying hither and yon. I walked around the entire bare spot, stopped and looked it over wistfully.

"Not enough seed," I pondered. There still was plenty of seed in the bag. And I still could see too much earth between the seeds on the ground. I went over that patch of dirt again, even followed up by flipping handfuls in some spots.

The sprinkler gave the whole backyard a good watering. That evening, as the sun was setting – not that the shaded patch of seed would have noticed – I looked it over. "This is going to be beautiful," I proudly told myself.

A couple weeks later, I was headed out the back door for work when something caught my eye. Something green. Ohmigosh!

"Hey, kids! Hey, Donna!" I shouted to the family with every bit as much excitement as a boy on Christmas morning.

Sure enough, my gift was under the tree – a short but thick crop of new, bright-green, absolutely stunning grass. I walked to the edge of the patio and looked from one end to the other, side to side and back again. I smiled; I know I smiled because I could feel it ripple throughout my body.

"It's just grass, Dad," one of my lovely but naïve children said.

I knew better.

I stopped and gazed upon that grass often the next several weeks. I simply admired it. "Did you see the grass today?" "Yeah, Dad. But it's just grass." The next two times I mowed, I didn't dare pass over the new growth with that vicious blade. It wasn't time yet. Finally, like taking my son for his first haircut, I cautiously, gently pushed the lawnmower over what had been mud just a few months earlier. I looked back. Perfect! Each blade stood at green attention, all the same height, in thick, close quarters. I glanced out at the area beneath the evergreen. Hey, not bad, I thought. But this spot here, this is beautiful.

Less than two months later, the spot was bare and dusty again.

An arid spring had moved into a dry, early summer. The heat had become extreme. Whatever water I gave that part of the yard, the roots of the shady great oak drank with the vigor of a construction worker at lunch time. The grass hadn't had time to develop roots, certainly not enough to battle the mature ones of the tree. It thinned, then disappeared altogether.

"Told you grass is supposed to be planted in the fall."

But ... but ... it had looked so good, so promising, so hopeful.

"It's only grass, Dad."

Autumn came and went. I was too busy to buy more seed and try again. Or maybe I was a bit downhearted. Or stubborn.

One Saturday the next spring, I grabbed my car keys. "Going to get some grass seed!" I shouted to Donna.

"Wait until October!" she hollered back.

I already had closed the door behind me.

During the winter, Trixie had worn the bare patch even larger. So the first thing I did when I got home was move her chain into an area where the lawn was strong. A further walk for us when we took her outside, but this grass would be worth the inconvenience.

I went about spreading the seed. Lots of seed. Back and forth, several times. Is that enough? This part needs more. And that part. I covered the area heavily. Donna asked if it might be too thick. It's fine. It's going to grow.

After pulling the hose out, I set the sprinkler on the far end and started to water it. As I did, I noticed another section of rather meager grass under the other side of the oak, next to the driveway. I had some leftover seed; I tossed it there. What the heck, I thought as I moved the sprinkler to that area later, it won't hurt to try.

I watered the new seed again the next evening. And the next, and the next. Almost every night through the dry spring. What's more, I would sit on a chair on the patio as the sprinkler did its work and I would recite my evening prayers, or settle into contemplative prayer, or simply enjoy the outdoors. I would admire the growth nearly every day, toss a handful of seed in areas that didn't seem to be faring so well, then methodically water it from top to bottom, side to side. I soaked it. You can have your drink, Big Tree, but I'm gonna make sure there's enough for these Little Guys.

I stood and coaxed, encouraged, sweet-talked, affirmed, enjoyed. It was some fine-looking grass, standing tall and green and proud – dare I say, it was almost luxuriant. Hey, Big Tree, you actually should revel in this soft, gorgeous carpeting on your floor. Say, family, come check out our yard now!

June passed. A tremendously dry June, but my watering and constant TLC kept the baby grass alive. Early July – danger! Dryness turned into drought, low-90s on the thermometer turned to high-90s. I watered all the more, prayed regularly, but things were starting to appear gloomy, even desperate. The green faded, some areas of dirt showed through the blades. My grass was leaner and leaner, thinning faster than a man who fell asleep in a sauna. One huge thunderstorm hit; the torrent of rain washed down the incline and wiped out more grass.

By mid-July, when a string of 100-degree days turned all outdoors into nothing but the constant humming of air-conditioners and the song of the locusts, my grass was nothing more than a memory. I tried, ridiculously, to rescue the dream. I turned on the sprinkler. The weeds were grateful. When my footsteps left deep impressions in mud where once had thrived the hope of fescue, I knew I had been licked again.

Not long afterward, while I was attending Mass, the priest remarked that he was wearing green vestments because it was the season of "Ordinary Time" on the liturgical calendar of the Catholic Church.

Green? Ordinary?

Obviously, church leaders never have tried to get grass to grow …

Speaking of calendars, it's October. I think I'll get my shovel. Clearly soil needs to be disturbed, shoveled and turned over, bothered and put through some anxiety before that little seed can turn into something truly inspiring. And then I'll get the spreader. After all, I always can buy more grass seed and find the hope that comes inside every bag.

Pray with me, please:

Father, all you want from me is my love and my trust – in you. Trust, that combination of faith and hope. Those are so hard to come by most days. So I ask of you now: Help my unbelief; give me faith. And where there only seems to be dirt and mud in my life, please plant hope. I want to feel the joy of trusting in you.

***   ***   ***   ***   ***

TAKING ACTION: Turn to this section near the back of the book. Find the action points that correspond with this chapter and try to commit yourself to following the suggestions.

CHAPTER TWELVE:

"THE BATTLE IS NOT YOURS"

"The Lord says to you: 'Do not fear or lose heart, for the battle is not yours but God's.... Take your places, stand firm, and see how the Lord will be with you to deliver you. Do not fear or lose heart.'"

Picture yourself in Jerusalem to behold the scene: In the sight of all his subjects, King Jehoshaphat just has meekly bowed down like one of his royal slaves and borne public witness to his weakness in the face of the gravest of dangers. The Hebrew people of the day believe that the greater a man's wealth, the greater his blessing and his favor in God's eyes. They look to their king for protection but also admire him and count upon him for security and for guidance.

Their enemies are fast approaching. Death hovers with an imminence.

Jehoshaphat guides them ... to look to God.

So here are thousands of men and women, maybe their children, all the servants and assistants and attendants to the king, his prophets and advisors – everyone staring in silence at the most powerful man of the nation lying prostrate and crying in desperate need that he has no answers, that he has no power, that all he can do is whisper toward the heavens "God, my eyes are turned toward you."

Out in the crowd, a young man named Jahaziel gazes in amazement along with everyone else. In the grace of the moment, Jahaziel hears God tell him something. Interesting, thinks Jahaziel, who feels a smile of joy bubbling somewhere inside but has a little doubt about the probability of such a marvelous answer to his king's prayer coming so quickly – and coming to *him*, of all people.

"No, really, Jahaziel," God tells him. "It's going to happen just as I have told you. Now, I want you to tell everyone else here."

"You want me to do what?!" Jahaziel responds. "I'm no speech-maker. I'm no prophet. I'm nothing special. Why are you telling all this to me?"

"Because I want to," God responds. "Because I want you."

"You want me?"

"Yes," God says. "I love you. I love all my people here. And I want to work through you, to tell Jehoshaphat and the others that they have done the right thing, that they have come to the right place. I want you to tell them that their faith in me has touched my heart."

By that time, Jahaziel has no choice. He is so overwhelmed by God's Presence, by God's love, by God's request, that he speaks up without noticing the looks of surprise on all his family and friends gathered around him.

"King Jehoshaphat!" Jahaziel says. "God wants me to tell you something. The Lord says, 'Do not fear or lose heart!'"

* * * * *

Bad things are going to happen in life. People unexpectedly will die in car accidents or of heart attacks, leaving our world before we get a chance to tell them how we feel about them and say good-bye. Cancer and AIDS will strike. Divorce will happen. Companies will lay off employees. Finances will get so tight that people will wonder how to pay the next bill that comes in the mail. Children will be born crippled or mentally handicapped.

Millions of people will suffer with severe depression every year. Sometimes, we will find an explanation, a "triggering event," as psychiatrists call it. Most times, there will be no clear answer, no external reason, and science might never understand the internal reasons for misfiring sections of the brain.

Jehoshaphat demonstrates that we don't have to look for an answer, that our response is what really matters. And among the many responses and actions we can take, one is most vital:

Turn to God.

And then get out of the way.

Cast your eyes and your cares upon Him, then simply and faithfully watch and wait. The darkness you feel is common and doesn't have to be frightening. God is there. That's one message found in the simply elegant and inspiring song "Sometimes By Step," written by the late Rich Mullins. In part he sang:

"And on this road to righteousness/Sometimes the climb can be so steep"

"I may falter in my steps/But never beyond your reach."

* * * * *

Almost every day during the last six years, I have wished depression never had arrived in my life. I spent some of that time wondering why life couldn't have stayed as it had been. I spent more of that time feeling guilty, as I looked at what damage had been done to me and especially to those whom I love. Often, I wanted to escape, to go somewhere I could be rid of the sense of failure and misery – and knowing there was only one ready means of escape. Most of the time, I tried to discern a way to live the life I had been given: to remain faithful to God, to be a good husband, parent and friend, to do my job well.

Sometimes, rare times to be sure, I actually thanked God for the depression. He has taught me so much in the darkness, things that I never could have learned with the depth of understanding I have now. Just as God rewarded King Jehoshaphat and his people with the opportunity to watch the defeat of their foes and then spend three days collecting booty from the dead, so has God given me some gifts during this battle.

I know the need for patience. Positive answers to our prayers might not come when we wish. God does his thing in the world and in molding the lives of people, but he does it in *his* time.

I not only know the need for humility, I have felt it become part of my life. No longer will I try to be Mr. Faultless, the man who can do everything exactly the right way and do it all by himself. God has blessed me with people who want to help; I'm able to accept their love.

I never even considered the importance of obedience before this disease. Now, I know there are things I am told to do that I have to do, directions I must follow. Before, I would follow directions because I was taught to do so, but I would disobey if I thought I knew a better way. I have come to understand that there are authorities who know more than I do, and I just yield obediently to their knowledge and authority – even moreso to God's direction.

I gradually have embraced a simplicity in life. Complications don't appeal to me. Give me the basics: family, friends, food, shelter, work, church. That's enough.

I have been blessed with a wisdom that I never knew before. Not intelligence; that's something different. That doesn't help you see through the clutter of life to what truly is significant.

I think this disease also has cultivated levels of compassion and mercy that go deeper than I ever imagined possible in myself. The pain of the world, in those people within my reach and those outside the realm of my everyday life, registers with me in a way that evokes sympathy and makes me want to help. I feel more tolerant of others different from me or those going through difficulties. Though never will I approach perfection, I find myself able to forgive more closely to the way I know God has forgiven me.

For all that I have "improved," I realize I am even further from the ideal place than I would have suspected six years ago.

None of those enhanced qualities have made me a person better than anyone else. I get impatient, with my disease and with others and with life in general. I struggle with bouts of pride. I don't always follow my doctor's directions or my wife's advice. I find that I wish I could make a little more money in order to pay off debt and maybe buy a new car, a new suit, a nice gift for a friend. I frequently overlook when those closest to me are hurting or need me in some way, and I'm usually not wise enough to know what to do to help ease their pain.

I can try to understand why God ever would allow this to happen to me, to us. I mean, I call him my Father. I know how much I love my children and that he loves me beyond any love I could even fathom. So how could God watch my body shudder from painful sobbing, me suffering to the core of my soul? How could he tolerate Donna going through such loneliness without the affectionate husband she needs, such frustration at not knowing how to help me? How could he permit my children to live without the fun, supportive, stable Dad they used to have? I have avoided friends at times, often frustrated their desire to help. My parents have had to watch their son and my family go through this and not know how to help. Finances have gotten so tight that we didn't know how we would make it through the month.

And we are only one family that has endured this. I know there are millions of people who undergo the same trials, and in many cases much, much worse.

God could solve it all in a snap. That's how I would have twisted the plot.

Thank goodness our God is smarter than me.

When each of my children was a baby, there came a point that we had to help them learn to sleep through the night. We had gotten into the habit of putting them to bed, then getting up when they awoke and cried for us every two or three hours. Sometimes, I would put my baby daughter or son on my shoulder, sit in the living room and sing to them softly as I rocked them back to sleep.

I loved to sing a few different things. *"Mommy loves Jessica. Daddy loves Jessica. Grandma loves Jessica. Grandpa loves Jessica. God loves Jessica. Everybody loves Jessica."* That was a standard.

And I liked this one a lot: *"I'll love you forever, I'll like you for always. As long as I am living, my baby you'll be." (By author Robert Munsch)*

There comes a time in each baby's life – and in each parent's life – when hard lessons have to be taught. So when they were a few months old and didn't need two or three nightly feedings, Donna and I decided we would have to refrain from picking them up. We would have to let them cry themselves back to sleep. I'll never forget those nights. I still can picture my son or daughter standing in their crib, crying and screaming, tears streaming down their cheeks and their eyes puffed with redness, calling out "Mommy! Daddy!" The entire time, Donna and I lay in our bed listening, praying, hurting. Several times, I got ready to give in, to get up and love them back to sleep. Donna would stop me. And I knew she was right. It just hurt so much to teach something important to my child in such an agonizing way.

I truly believe God watches those of us affected by depression and cries with us, hurts with us, might even have moments when he wants to step in and stop it. Yet in his great wisdom, the Lord knows that we will be all right and that he wants to use the time to make our lives even better by teaching us to depend more than ever on him.

God has shown me the merit of all those qualities. What's more, he has shown me that achieving any of those virtues is impossible without him – not really *our* achievements but his. I want to depend upon the Almighty God completely. His patience allows me to be a work-in-progress, but the more of myself I surrender to him, the more patient a man I will be. The more obedient I will become in answering his call. The more detached I will be from things of this world, which will pass away, and more attached I will be to things of heaven.

I now daily say a prayer, written by the late Thomas Merton, which says in part:

"Therefore will I trust you always though I may seem to be lost and in the shadow of death.

"I will not fear, for you are ever with me, and you will never leave me to face my perils alone."

I still feel lost most days. I still find myself shivering in the cold of the shadow of death, which makes me concerned. But I have learned that I need not be afraid, because more than ever my depression has taught me that all that really matters is not that I please God in all that I do, but that I *want* to please Him.

Yes, sometimes the climb is unbearably steep and we feel we can't keep going. And even if we do keep going, we still may falter in our steps.

But no matter how hard we fall, how desperate we may feel in the throes of our deepest depression, we never are beyond our

Father's reach.

Are you powerless and feel like you don't know what to do? Then join Jehoshaphat in praying, "Hence, my eyes are turned toward You."

And know that God has been looking at you, and loving you, the whole time.

Pray with me, please:

Thank you, my God, for loving me.

***   ***   ***   ***   ***

TAKING ACTION: Turn to this section near the back of the book. Find the action points that correspond with this chapter and try to commit yourself to following the suggestions.

TAKING ACTION

I am the first to acknowledge that asking a victim of major depression to take on a burdensome plan toward managing his disease is unwise and absurdly ambitious at the least, and at its worst, dangerous. I also know that "burdensome" can be a relative idea; some of the simplest actions for healthy people can feel insurmountable to someone with the disease.

Nonetheless, I want to make some suggestions. They are organized by chapter. Perhaps some loved one can help the sufferer look at each chapter and set priorities, decide which one or two seem feasible at least to attempt. Try to make the suggestions of Chapter One part of your life for one week, then add the suggestions of Chapter Two the second week, and so on. Don't replace the previous week's suggestions, add to them. And if it seems too much, then don't add anything new until you feel ready.

You have nothing to lose but misery.

CHAPTER ONE:

- Question to ponder: Do you feel God has let you down?

- Write down this version of The Prayer of Jehoshaphat:

See how this roaring lion is coming at me. Oh God, will you not get rid of it? I am powerless against it. I am at a loss what to do, hence my eyes are turned toward you."

Place a copy where you will see it every day – by your alarm clock, on the mirror of your bathroom, next to your purse or wallet or car keys. Recite it at least twice each day, once in the morning and once at night, no matter how you are feeling that day.

- Memorize this part of Jehoshaphat's prayer: "I am powerless against it. I'm at a loss what to do, hence my eyes are turned toward you." Repeat it frequently during the day, especially when you are taking your medication or when you feel particularly bad.

CHAPTER TWO:

- Questions to ponder: Do you blame yourself for your depression? Do you blame God perhaps for allowing it or sending it to you? What will it take for someone to convince you that depression is a disease and not a punishment for something you have done?

- Talk about your faith with someone. Share with them the

strongest aspect and weakest aspect. Recite with them The Lord's Prayer. Commit to saying that prayer, slowly, at least twice each day.

- Purchase a small notebook; I like those "Marble Memo" booklets, because they are sturdy and small enough to keep in a pocket or purse. Occasionally during the week, write several things into the notebook. Perhaps a verse from Scripture. A brief prayer or quote that has resonated with you. Consider this the beginning of your "Prayer Gems." Use one of the pages to jot this line in particular: "Lord, please be my strength in my weakness." Whenever you find your depression beginning to devour you, pray those words.

CHAPTER THREE:

- Every time you are outdoors, look at the sky. Cloudy or sunny, day or night, starry with a clear moon or ready to storm. Just look at it.

- Write a few more Scripture verses, short prayers and quotes in your "Prayer Gems." Occasionally during the day, either at a most challenging time or when you feel stronger than usual, open the booklet, read a page that has meaning in the moment and reflect on that brief reading.

CHAPTER FOUR:

- Question to ponder: Do you ever simply cry to the Lord for help?

- Are you named after a saint? Or do you have a favorite saint? If not, choose Saint Francis of Assisi or Saint Clare. Read about them. Ask them to pray for you.

- Bookmark in your Bible these selections: Psalms 25, 27, 51, 104 and 108. Read just one of them each day. After you have looked them over a few times, you will get a sense of the unique nature of each. Then, whatever mood you find yourself in that day, read that Psalm. And every day, read Psalm 117. It has only two verses. But commit to saying it every single day, no matter how you feel.

- Continue your time adding to your "Prayer Gems" and reflecting on something from that notebook regularly. Try to make both exercises a daily practice.

CHAPTER FIVE:

- Take a few moments each day this week – maybe you start out with only three minutes and then work your way up to a few more – and simply ask God to be with you. Don't ask Him to do anything or tell you anything. Don't spend the time complaining to Him. Just ask Him to be with you. Turn off the TV and radio. Don't answer the phone if it rings. Simply be quiet.

- Continue your time adding to your "Prayer Gems" and reflecting on something from that notebook regularly.

CHAPTER SIX:

- Question to ponder: Have you ever considered meeting regularly with someone to discuss your faith honestly, openly yet confidentially (if need be) at least on a monthly basis? With whom could you spend time discussing your faith – not your disease? What would you like to share?

- Put together a team. Find a psychiatrist you feel you trust to make good medication recommendations. Find a psychologist with whom you are comfortable talking about your life and your depression. If your first choice doesn't feel right, look for another. Think about at least one friend and one family member whom you trust enough to share what's happening with you.

- Continue your time adding to your "Prayer Gems" and reflecting on something from that notebook regularly.

CHAPTER SEVEN:

- On those days when you don't feel like talking with anyone or even leaving the house, don't allow it to be a completely wasted day. Find at least one task you can do, such as empty the dishwasher or wipe off the sink in the bathroom. And find at least one thing to read, whether it is a short chapter in a book or an article in a magazine. Two small things, but don't go an entire day holed up away from the world without doing at least two small things.

- Find a spiritual director, someone who won't judge your beliefs but will help guide your heart in whatever direction the Lord is calling you. Meet with that person at least once a month.

- Continue your time adding to your "Prayer Gems" and reflecting on something from that notebook regularly.

CHAPTER EIGHT:

- Brief questions to ponder for each day of the week. Don't judge yourself or your answers, just honestly reflect on them:

  Monday – What if your depression persists for an extended period: how will you feel about that and react to it?

  Tuesday – Why will you not allow some people who offer to help you to actually help you?

  Wednesday – Do you follow all the instructions of your psychiatrist and psychologist, and if not, why not?

  Thursday – How much time do you spend daily in prayer, and what do you enjoy about your prayer?

Friday – What assistance have you enlisted that can help treat your disease, and if you have avoided some suggestions, why?

Saturday – How do you react when others in your life need some kind of help, or do you even notice?

Sunday – How completely have you forgiven yourself for things you have done or haven't done, especially during this time of depression, and how completely do you feel God has forgiven you?

- Sing a song. Every day. Something that makes you cry or something that makes you smile or something that helps you to pray. Whatever it is, sing it. One suggestion is "Day By Day," from Godspell. You probably won't feel like doing it regularly, so on days when you can't muster the strength or desire, then hum it. But do it every single day.

- Continue your time adding to your "Prayer Gems" and reflecting on something from that notebook regularly.

CHAPTER NINE:

- Write down four names: Two of them among your closest friends, two of them family members you trust. Call each and ask if they have a few minutes. Then tell them what it is that they do for you that you most appreciate and ask if they could help you by doing that more often for a while.

- Continue your time adding to your "Prayer Gems" and reflecting on something from that notebook regularly.

CHAPTER TEN:

- Question to ponder: What do you think you have learned about yourself and your relationship with God during your time of depression?

- Look to God. Find a way to focus all your attention upon Him. Start with one minute. Tell God that you are willing to acknowledge that you are completely dependent upon Him. Don't listen for answers to your problems. Don't ask for anything. Just sit and tell God that all you want to do is look at Him.

- Continue your time adding to your "Prayer Gems" and reflecting on something from that notebook regularly.

CHAPTER ELEVEN:

- Think about something in life that gives you hope, something you can think about every day. Write it down. Put that piece of paper next to wherever you keep your copy of The Prayer of Jehoshaphat, and think about that hopeful feeling regularly.

- Continue your time adding to your "Prayer Gems" and reflecting on something from that notebook regularly.

CHAPTER TWELVE:

- Question to ponder: What kind of person do you hope you will be once your depression eases? What have you learned to help you become that person?

- Make a list tonight of three good things that happened today. They might not be big things. You drank a glass of juice, which is good for your health. A friend called. You got out of bed. You made it through the day. Three good things. Write them down tonight. Then do it again tomorrow night. And the next night.

- This might be the most challenging of all the suggestions you will hear: Thank God for your depression and the things you have learned because of it. Make yourself say it, to recite your gratitude to God frequently each day.

SOURCES AND REFERENCES

* All Biblical quotations and references from "The New American Bible, St. Joseph Edition," published by Catholic Book Publishing, 1991 update edition.

* Bodo, Murray. "The Journey and The Dream," about Saint Francis of Assisi. It's an interesting book that is less a true biography of the venerable saint as it is an opportunity to reflectively experience some of what St. Francis experienced.

* Bowden, Malcolm. Author of the website www.mbowden.surf3.net. Bowden is a consulting civil and structured engineer, head of the Association of True Biblical Counselors and author of four books on creationism. He also co-authored "Breakdowns Are Good For You" with Dr. Robert Law.

* Center for the Development of Peace and Well-Being, University of California-Berkeley.

* Enterline, Jim. Author of the online Select Christian Resources newsletter. He has been "ministering to the hurting and addicted" through Jesus 2 U Ministries since 1992.

* Information about saints from www.americancatholic.org.

* Goldman, L.S.; Nielsen, N.H., and Champion, H.C., authors of "Awareness, diagnosis and treatment of depression," produced for the Council on Scientific Affairs and published in the Journal of General Internal Medicine, September 1999.

* Lloyd-Jones, Dr. Martin. Author of the book "Spiritual Depression." Lloyd-Jones occasionally is harsh in his advice for depression victims, but he does point out that many victims will need medication to help them through the most difficult times and that effective psychotherapy is necessary.

* Longman, Robert Jr. Author of an article entitled "The Fruit of the Spirit" on www.spirithome.com in March 2003.

* Manning, Brennan. Author of the book "The Ragamuffin Gospel." This is a must-read for any Christian seeking to understand the full extent of the grace and salvation God offers.

* McManamy, John. Author of the article "When Your Brain Goes Crash" on his website www.mcmanweb.com. He also is the author of the book "Living Well with Depression and Bipolar Disorder."

* Merton, Thomas. Selection from his book "Thoughts in Solitude." Frankly, anything written by Merton is worth reading, and I have grown immensely more intimate in my relationship with God because of Merton.

* Morris, Grantley. Author of the website www.net-burst.net, which

has the stated mission of "ministering to the hurting" and "helping millions of Christians and not-yet-Christians fall more in love with Jesus."

* Mullins, Mary. Author of the website www.circleofprayer.com.

* Mullins, Rich. Excerpts from a series of interviews compiled by radio program "20: The Countdown Magazine." Lyrics from his song "Sometimes By Step," written by Rich Mullins and Beaker, copyright 1992 Edward Grant Inc. Rich died in a car accident in September 1997; I miss Rich every single day. I thank God for the music he gave us while here on earth, and I recommend his albums to anyone who appreciates good music – he was a supremely gifted musician and songwriter. But his songs also will help you love God more deeply and in ways you never expected.

* New Advent Catholic Encyclopedia.

* Pocket Catholic Dictionary, by John A. Hardon S.J. and published by The Real Presence Association, Chicago, Ill..

* Richmond, Raymond Lloyd Ph.D. Author of the website www.chastitysf.com.

* Saint John of the Cross, "Dark Night of the Soul." This book isn't for young Christians. But if you wish to explore contemplative prayer as a way of greater intimacy with God, this is a must-read.

* Solomon, Andrew. Author of the extremely thorough and insightful book "The Noonday Demon" and the essay "Anatomy

of Melancholy." Probably the best book I read about depression. I would caution you that it's a big book and includes some indepth (although interesting) sections on the history of treatment of depression and how the disease shows up in different cultures; that might seem tedious at times to someone who doesn't feel like reading much. Solomon is a supremely gifted albeit occasionally high-brow writer. But I can imagine many depression sufferers will read his experience of depression and exclaim, "Finally! Someone has put into words what I feel."

* Swindoll, Charles. Selections from his book "Paul: A Man of Grace and Grit." I'm a big fan of almost anything Swindoll has written. But this book, part of a series about Biblical figures, provided many great lessons in highly readable form.

* Timmerman, John. He is a professor of English at Calvin College in Grand Rapids, Mich., and wrote "A Season of Suffering," published by Multnomah in 1988. Selections used connected to Timmerman and his wife Pat's journal are from an article that appeared in the March 2, 1988, edition of Christian Century. I recommend caretakers and friends of depression victims read the selections from Pat's journal.

* Tully, the Rev. William. He was a rector at St. Bartholomew's Church in New York City when he delivered a sermon Dec. 12,

2004, with depression as a teaching theme.

* Whybrow, Peter and Bahr, Robert. Authors of "The Hibernation Response." Other hibernation research courtesy of a study by the University of Texas Health Science Center at Houston.

* Wolf Shenk, Joshua. Author of the article "Lincoln's Great Melancholy," published in The Atlantic, October 2005. An amazing book that looks at the extent of Abraham Lincoln's depression. The man already is one of the most admirable men in American history. Read this and you will find you admire him even more.

* Huber, Cheri. "The Depression Book: Depression as an Opportunity for Spiritual Growth." Published by Keep It Simple Books, 2004.

* Chambers, Oswald. "My Utmost For His Highest." Published by Christian Art Books, 2002.

* Websites www.nami.org (National Alliance on Mental Illness), www.nimh.nih.gov (National Institute of Mental Health) and www.mayoclinic.com provide great, up-to-date information.

* Quotations of Robert Frost, Matthew Kelty, Theodore Roethke, T.S. Eliot, Tom Stewart and Soren Kierkegaard gleaned from a variety of on-line quote services.